Benjamin Vaughan Abbott

The travelling law-school and Famous trials

Benjamin Vaughan Abbott

The travelling law-school and Famous trials

ISBN/EAN: 9783337210601

Printed in Europe, USA, Canada, Australia, Japan

Cover: Foto ©Suzi / pixelio.de

More available books at **www.hansebooks.com**

BUSINESS BOYS' LIBRARY.—II.

The Travelling Law-School

AND

FAMOUS TRIALS

(First Lessons in Government and Law)

BY

BENJAMIN VAUGHAN ABBOTT

order to succeed in life you must resolve to carry into your work a fulness of knowledge."— President ⬛⬛⬛

BOST⬛
LOTHROP A⬛
FRANKLIN ⬛

CONTENTS.

THE TRAVELLING LAW SCHOOL.

FAMOUS TRIALS.

5

THE TRAVELLING LAW-SCHOOL.

I. — THE STATE-HOUSE AT BOSTON.

" National powers and State powers " is an incomplete classification. Our fathers carefully divided all governmental powers into three classes; one they gave to the States; another to the nation; but the third great class, comprising the most precious of all powers, they refused to confer on the State or nation, but reserved to themselves. GARFIELD—*Chips from the White House*, p. 443.

ALMOST everywhere in America there are three governments. One good way for young citizens to learn about them is to take a journey, observing, on the way, whether the things they pass are subject to one government or to another. The Statehouse in Boston will be a good place for beginning such a journey; for in visiting a State-house we learn about the State government. Then if we travel to Washington, we shall there see something of what is done by the government of the United States. While travelling, instead of watching for beautiful scenery or remarkable buildings, we must look for the changes in governments and laws.

7

"Please, sir, may girls go ? "

Certainly. They will be very welcome. They shall·have seats by the windows and ask all the questions they wish. Even if girls should never vote, they need to know about governments and laws, in order to understand the news they read, and to converse with gentlemen about " politics," and to manage their own property.

Now for the reason for having three governments:ʼ It is that they may take care of different things. We might almost say that the United States government — or, as it is sometimes called, the Federal or National government—has charge of the largest things; the State governments, of medium-sized things ; while small matters are regulated by some kind of corporation. The words small and large are not very good. A letter, folded in its envelope, is small ; yet letters are managed by the United States. A park like Fairmount, or Central, or the Boston Common, is large, yet it is managed by the corporation of the city. But the idea is, that although any one letter is small, yet the business of carrying letters over the whole country and sending them to foreign lands is a very large thing; too large for a corporation or even a State. Grown persons, instead of using "large" and "small," would perhaps say, The United States government controls *national* subjects, and the State those which are of *general* interest to one community; while merely *local* affairs are directed by some corporation. On our journey we shall better see what this means.

Now our party is gathered at the State-house. What can we learn about State governments by examining a State-house? A great deal. Any State-house is built to provide rooms for doing the business of the State government. There are now thirty-eight States, and each needs a "house" for its business. The pictures of these houses would appear very different; but the arrangements of the rooms and the nature of the business done in them is much the same. The most important rooms are those of the legislature. The legislature is composed of gentlemen elected by the people throughout the State, to meet at the State-house and make laws for the State. They are entirely distinct from the United States government. Part of them are called "the Senate," the other part "the House of Representatives," or sometimes "the Assembly." The Senate and the House have each a room in the State-house, arranged much like a school-room, but larger and more elegant. The floors of these rooms are occupied with handsome desks and chairs, at which the members of the legislature sit, listening to each other's speeches, or reading or writing — much like the pupils in a school. At a large desk on a raised platform sits a president or speaker, and near him are clerks ; looking like a principal and assistant teachers. There usually is what is not so common in school-rooms — a gallery for visitors. Whenever any person wishes a new State law he must wait until the legislature is in session (for legislatures have vacations, as do schools), and must bring it to be proposed to the members of the House or the Senate, sitting in one of these halls. A written paper proposed for a law is called a "bill." A clerk will read the bill, so that the members can hear it ; and they, if they like it, will give it to a "committee" for examination. A committee in a legislature resembles a class in a school : it consists of perhaps five, or seven, or nine members, who carry the proposed law into a side room like a recitation room, and there study it. The purpose of their studying is to judge whether the law will be a good one. Afterwards they "report" to the other members in the large hall what they have learned about the bill, and whether or not they recommend it. Any member who pleases may make a speech in favor of the bill or against it. Then the president or speaker says: "All who are in favor of this bill say 'Aye;' contrary minded, 'No.'" If enough members vote "Aye," the bill is "passed" along to the members sitting in the other hall, where it is discussed and voted upon in the same way. If enough members in the other house vote "Aye," the bill is "passed" along to the Governor. This is what is meant by saying "a bill was passed."

The Governor is the chief officer of the State. He has a spacious room in the capitol, near the legislative halls, and whenever a bill has been passed it is brought to him. If he thinks it good, he marks it "approved;" and by this mark it becomes a law. Besides approving laws, each Governor has a great deal of business to manage for his State. He can forbid laws which he sees to be unwise; and can pardon criminals and set them free. He appoints various officers and gives orders; and if any officer neglects his duty, the Governor calls him to account. He does not take regular vacations like the legislature, but attends to business at any time; and very responsible and difficult business it is.

In any State-house there are, besides the legislative halls, the committee rooms and the "executive chamber," as the Governor's room is often called, and many other business rooms. The most interesting one is the State library. One can enjoy many days in examining and reading the curious books. There are also, usually, some paintings, statues and curiosities : thus at the State-house in Boston are statues of Washington, Webster and Mann; busts of Adams, Lincoln and Andrew; and flags carried by Massachusetts regiments in the civil war. And if we ascend to the great gilded dome, there is a beautiful view of Boston and of the country around. Even persons who are not interested in laws and governments take pleasure in visiting a State-house, as there is so much to be seen which is elegant and curious.

One of the pleasures of educated persons in journeying abroad lies in comparing foreign forms of government with ours. Probably no European country has adopted the three governments as distinctly as we have. Great Britain is formed by a union of kingdoms — England, Scotland, Ireland — somewhat like our States, and has colonies somewhat like our Territories. Parliament is like our Congress, and the three kingdoms send representatives to it; but then they have no legislatures of their own. The large colonies have legislatures, but are not represented in Parliament. England has counties, cities and towns, however: indeed, it was from these that America took the idea.

Switzerland strongly resembles the United States. There is a Diet resembling our Congress, and there are Cantons, like our States. But the Cantons differ much more than do our States in their ways of managing their local governments. In the Diet the Cantons are represented in a manner which, while giving in the House deputies similar to our representatives, in proportion to the number of voters, equalizes the Cantons in the Senate. But in the Cantons themselves there are all varieties of republican governments. In some Cantons the voters elect only the officers of the great council; the grand council chooses the chief executive, who is called Avoyer, Landaman, or Burgomaster, and corresponds to our Governor. In some Cantons the laws framed by the legislative assembly must be submitted to the people. In others, the people are periodically convened to vote directly on the public business, much as is the way in a New England town meeting.

NOTE. — For description of the English form of government, read Stubb's "Constitutional History of England," "Anecdotal History of Parliament," Green's "Shorter History of the English People." "Switzerland," page 553 (Lothrop's "Library of Entertaining History ") gives a clear account of the Swiss Diet and Cantons,

II.—THINGS ONE CAN OWN.

" Property is the fruit of labor; property is desirable, is a positive good in the world. That some should be rich shows that others may become rich, and hence is just encouragement to independence and enterprise." LINCOLN : *Chips from the White House,* page 262.

PROPERTY is a difficult word. One way of learning its meanings is to read them in dictionaries and cyclopædias. For the Travelling Law-school a better way is to take notice of the various kinds of property we see. A city like Boston contains a great many different kinds. And all useful things are not "property." Air is not considered property, neither is light; though they are absolutely necessary. There was once a large and expensive store built by the side of a beautiful garden. It was somewhat dark and close, and the shop-keeper cut some windows in the side wall to let light and air into the store from above the garden. The owner

15

of the garden asked the court to forbid this. "I cannot," said the judge; "the shop-keeper is only cutting holes in his own wall; he has the right to do that."

Said the garden owner, "But he is stealing the light and air above my garden."

"No," said the judge, "the light and air over your garden are not your *property*. While they are over it you can use them; but if they fly off and enter your neighbor's windows it is not stealing for him to use them."

Then the gardener returned home, and began building a wall on the edge of the garden, up — up — till it was covering the windows. The owner of the store then asked the court to forbid this wall. "I cannot," said the judge; "he is only building a wall on his own land; he has the right to do that."

Said the garden owner, "You decided that I had the right to cut windows."

"So you have," said the judge. "You have the right to have windows on your land, and he has the right to build a wall on his."

"But he is stealing the light and air from my windows."

"It is not stealing," said the judge, "to obstruct
light or air, for neither is property."

If this had happened in England, the judge would
have asked, "How old are the windows?" And
if they had been built more than twenty years he
would have called them "ancient lights," and would
have forbidden the building of the wall against them.
But in most parts of this country ancient windows
have no better right than those newly built.

Probably the chief reason why air and light are
not property is that there is no need and no way
of doing either up in parcels so that any particular quantity can be kept separate. A chief
idea of property is, *something that can be measured in
quantities for sale.* This cannot be done with natural air and light: how then can they be property?
But the gas used in cities for lighting is made in a
great retort, and runs in large pipes underground to
the various buildings, and in each building it runs
through a meter which measures every cubic foot, and
then through small pipes to burners in the rooms;
and there, when a screw is turned, it rushes out and
one can light it with a match. A man once contrived

to get gas for his house without paying, by boring a hole into the large gas-pipe and inserting a small pipe which brought some into his house. This house was in Ashland street in Boston. The gas company prosecuted the man for stealing. Said he, " It is not stealing, for gas is only a kind of air : now air is not property."

But the judges said that air manufactured to be burned and kept stored in tanks or pipes is property, and taking it without leave is stealing. If two divers went down, carrying each a tank of air to breathe, the air which each carried would be his property ; the other could not lawfully take it from him. Some person has said that he has invented a kind of wall paper which during the daytime will absorb the light and at night will give it out ; the wall will shine so that one can read by its light. When this is accomplished the light stored in a roll of such paper will be property.

Is water property ? When it has been gathered in casks or in bottles, as Congress water is, so that it can be carried to and fro, it is. When it is running in a stream, it is not; the person who owns the land

through which the stream runs has the right to use
it : for example, he can build a dam and use the
water to turn a mill-wheel ; but he must let it run on
its way down the stream, so that all who live below
can use it for their mills if they desire. In winter,
when the water of great rivers and ponds freezes, the
ice is free to every one until some one has begun
gathering it ; as fast as any one takes particular ice it
becomes his property. One winter some ice gath-
erers selected a spot on the frozen surface of the
Mississippi where the ice was clear and good, and
marked corners with stakes, and plowed a line
around a quantity which they thought would be
enough to fill their ice-house. They placed a watch-
man in charge of it until a good day came for cutting
it into blocks and carting it home. They then went
to cut it ; but a rival dealer accompanied by fifty
men armed with clubs, ice-picks and pistols, came to
the place, drove away the first party, and cut and carried away the ice themselves. When they were prosecuted, they said, "Ice is not property."

But the court said, "The surface of a great river is
free to all ; and whoever marks a plot of ice for mar-

ket becomes entitled to it as the first comer."

The land, and the buildings of which we see so many in a great city, are property; and this kind is so important that it is called *real estate*, or *real* property. The land belongs to some owner, even in wild and desolate places where there are no fences nor any cultivation. If not a part of any one's farm, still there is some one who owns it, or it belongs to one of the governments; the town or county, or the State, or the United States. No one has the right to take land for his own as he may ice in a river, merely because it is wild and unoccupied. One who tries to do this is called a "squatter." The land surely belongs to some one, although to find the true owner is sometimes difficult. So many people wish to live in the cities that the land becomes very valuable and the buildings are placed very close together. The buildings are considered part of the land, because they are built on foundations planted in the ground, and cannot be moved away. Property which can be moved from place to place, such as the furniture in the houses, the merchandise in the stores, and the vehicles in the streets, is called *personal* property, or sometimes *chattels*. Almost any grown person can explain about owning land or buildings, and about hiring them ; also about chattels and how these are bought and sold. One curious rule is that the real property is subject to the law of the State where it lies; the land and the buildings in Boston must be sold or hired according to the law of Massachusetts, no matter where the owner lives. But chattels or personal property are subject to the law of the State where the owner of them resides. Another curious rule is, that if one wishes to sell real property it is necessary that he should give a *deed*. When chattels are sold, no written paper is necessary; for example, one can enter a store, select an article, pay the price, and, if the merchant delivers the thing to him to take away, or sends it home, it becomes the property of the buyer merely by this "delivery." Not so when one wishes to buy houses and lands. He needs a deed. A deed is a long paper, partly printed and partly written, which gives the names of the seller and the buyer, and describes the land very carefully, and the buildings, and says that they have been sold for such and such a price. So also if one wishes to hire a farm or a house, unless the time is very short, he must take from the owner a *lease* stating very distinctly what property he is to hire, how long he may keep it, and what the rent is to be.

Are animals property? There are two kinds. Domestic animals, such as horses, cows, sheep, hens, are property. In some States dogs are property, in some they are not. Wild beasts and birds in the woods, or fishes in the sea, do not belong to any one ; if, however, a person catches one it is his property for the time being; but if it escapes and is at large again, the property of the one who first caught it is lost, and any one may take it. If my horse strays away he belongs to me wherever he goes. But if I have a menagerie and the lion breaks loose, any one may shoot him. Whether any one may catch and keep him is, perhaps, a knotty question. A hunter once shot at a deer in the woods and wounded it. The deer ran and the hunter with his dog followed until night. Next morning the hunter resumed the chase and tracked the deer to a spot where it had been killed by another man. The court said that the creature belonged to the hunter who killed it at last, for it had escaped from the other. In England a man lately set a carrier pigeon free, hoping it would fly home as he had trained it to do. On its way some person shot it, and, when he was sued, said, "That bird was not property, for the owner had turned it loose." But the judge said, "It is the nature of a carrier pigeon to fly home; the owner did not turn it loose because he did not value it, but to let it fly home; and it was property while on the way."

III.—THE CITY STREETS; AND THE DEPOT.

"The germ of our political institutions, the primary cell from which they were evolved, was in the New England town, and the vital force, the informing soul of the town, was the Town Meeting, which, for all local concerns, was king, lords and commons in all."—GARFIELD: *Chips from the White-house*, p. 458.

THE Travelling Law-school is now walking through Boston Common and along the city streets, on its way to the railroad depot. One pleasure in teaching American Little Citizens is that they know so many things at the start. All girls and boys know well enough what a city is, and that a city has laws of its own. Therefore the teacher will simply ask that one or two of the boys will keep watch for any city law which the party may pass; and meantime he will relate the story of the two dancing bears in Madison. The man who owned these bears brought them to the city of Madison to exhibit them. But he had learned that in any city there are laws about exhibitions, and that he must get leave before he could open a show. Therefore he went to the mayor's office and asked for a "permit." Every city has a mayor, some man whom the people choose to administer the city laws. His office is the place for obtaining permission to do anything extraordinary in a city; except that in very large cities there are several officers instead of only one. At the mayor's office the clerks gave the showman a permit. He then led his bears upon the sidewalk of the chief street, and told them to dance. They began, and a crowd gathered to see. Just then a man in a buggy, driving a spirited, skittish horse, came around the corner. When the horse saw the bears he was frightened; he ran away, the buggy was upset, and the driver was thrown out and badly hurt. The driver brought a lawsuit against the city, to be paid for being hurt. And the judges said that if the city officers had been so foolish as to tell the showman he might let his bears dance on the sidewalk of that crowded street, the city ought to pay damages; bears ought to be exhibited in a hired hall, or in a tent on some vacant lot. Thus we see that there must be rules in a city very different from those in the country. In the wild woods bears may roam where they please. And if a farmer should catch one and get a chain around him he might lead him across the fields to his house without harm being done. But in a city there is need of laws and officers to say exactly where and how bears — or other dangerous things, such as steam-engines, or gunpowder — may be carried or used.

"Please, sir, there is a city law."

"Where? Yes; that is one."

KEEP OFF THE GRASS.

It would be absurd for a legislature at a State-house to pass a law ordering the people to keep off the grass everywhere in the State. In country places walking in the fields may be perfectly proper. In a city park the grass must be protected; therefore the city officers are allowed to decide what the rule about walking on the grass in that city shall be. Just so it is their duty to decide where there shall be streets, and whether they shall be paved; to provide fire-engines and employ firemen for extinguishing fires ; to make arrangements for bringing in water by an aqueduct; and for lighting the streets with gas or electric light; and for like things which are important to all the people of the city, but do not concern the rest of the State.   They also employ policemen to set any one right who has lost his way, assist any one who is hurt, and prevent any one from doing mischief. All judicious and well-educated persons who visit a city are careful to obey all the city laws, and to comply with any directions which the policemen give them.

A few years ago on this very Boston Common, the city officers made a coasting place in the winter for the boys of the city.   They set apart a path which ran down hill for the coasting, and poured water over it to freeze and make the path slippery, and then stationed a police officer at the lower end to say to any one walking that way, "This is not a path for walking: it is the boys' coasting place."   Notwithstanding these things a grown man persisted in walking on that path.   The sled of a boy who was sliding down the hill ran against him, and he was knocked down and badly hurt.   He brought a law-

suit against the city to require the city to pay his
doctor's bill.   But the court said that the city had a
perfect right to make a coasting place for the boys;
and grown persons had no right to walk upon it.

Besides cities there are counties.   These have
charge of matters which are important in country
places where perhaps there may not be many people
living.   For example, the paved streets in a city are
usually made and kept in order by the city officers;
but the country roads which spread everywhere, running from one city or town to another, also the
bridges across streams, are usually made by the county
authorities.   The sign often posted over a bridge,
" Five dollars fine for driving across this bridge faster
than a walk," is an example of a county law.   And
counties have most to do with catching criminals;
for these might easily escape from the cities, and the
policemen could not be spared to search the woods
and fields for them.

Besides cities and counties there are towns and
villages.   It is, however, very difficult to explain
about these, because the words about them are not
used alike in all parts of the land.   Ask some grown

person to explain a good map of a State. It ought
to be a pretty large-sized map. On such a map you
will often find large irregular patches printed in different colors or with borders of different colors:
these are the counties. Every county is divided by
fine lines into little squares: these are towns or
townships. They are usually pretty square, but not
perfectly; in the Western States they are much more
regular and even than in the Eastern. Also here and
there little spots are marked, some large and black,
others smaller; some of these are called towns,
others are cities or villages. You will see that the
largest of these are in places convenient for ships
and railroads. You will see also that the counties fill
the entire State. So do the townships. But the
cities and villages do not fill the State: they are seen
only here and there where a great many persons wish
to live together. Usually, as soon as people begin to
live in a State in numbers, the whole State is divided
into counties, and again into townships, so that
every place can have some laws as fast as needed.
In these townships or towns all the inhabitants, so
long as there are not too many, meet in a public

meeting now and then, and make what laws they
please. They can make laws for their own town
only. Their assembly is called the town meeting.
When, however, so many persons reside in a place
that the town meeting becomes too large, the legislature sitting in the State-house will pass a law declaring that place a city. In a city there are no town
meetings; the inhabitants elect a mayor and some
aldermen to attend to the public business for them. '
A city hall is built, which corresponds to a State-
house. The mayor and aldermen meet here and decide questions or pass laws for the city. The meeting which makes laws for a city is often called the
common council.

The ancient cities of Europe began somewhat differently. The land was divided into small territories — kingdoms they were often called. Each kingdom was ruled by a king (or possibly a queen). He
was usually a military chieftain. Either he or one
of his ancestors had conquered the kingdom and divided the land among his soldiers ; and as the original
soldiers died their sons inherited the lands. Each king
was accustomed to require the inhabitants, in return for

his protecting them in their lands, to give part of their crops for the support of the king and his court and army officers; whenever he became engaged in war and needed soldiers, they were obliged to serve; also he would require the common people to pay tribute. Merchants and manufacturers disliked to be called away from their business to serve the king, or to have their profits consumed in tributes; hence they would often gather in a convenient spot, build a wall around it to keep out invaders, and declare themselves to be a city, and claim liberty to make their own laws. How far they could prove themselves to be free from the exactions of the kings and chieftains differed in different cities. But on the whole, a great deal of modern liberty was attained in this way, by the wiser, thriftier and more resolute people in the land combining in cities to resist the military tyranny of the soldiers, and to establish just laws.

But by this time we have reached the railroad depot. Now we shall begin a ride. We shall be in charge of the railroad corporation. The railroad companies make certain laws — regulations, they are usually called, and travellers need to understand and obey them.

IV. — PEOPLE WHOM WE MEET.

" If you should ever come to Cambridge, or near headquarters, I shall be happy to see a person so favored by the Muses, and to whom nature has been so liberal and beneficient." — WASHINGTON: *Chips from the White House*, p. 22.

"The Indians shall have my first attention ; and I will not rest until they shall have justice." — LINCOLN : *Id.* p. 283.

" Other nations see their people going, going. We see from every quarter the people of other countries, coming, coming, coming."—HAYES: *Id.* p. 373.

" No child of mine shall ever be *compelled* to study one hour, or to learn even the English alphabet, before he has deposited under his skin at least seven years of muscle and bone." — GARFIELD: *Id.* p. 408.

WHO would guess that the polite invitation above quoted was written to a slave girl ? It was. Her name was Phillis Wheatley. She addressed a complimentary poem to General Washington, and he wrote to thank her for it. His whole letter is given in *Chips*. It shows that even a hundred years ago wise and good men were willing to treat colored people kindly and politely. Yet many of the States held them in slavery. At length a great war arose, the result of which was that slavery was abolished forever. Ask some grown person to tell you about the war and emancipation. There are no slaves to be seen on the journey from the State-house at Boston to the capitol at Washington, but we shall meet many negroes. In the whole land there are about four million negroes. Almost all were born in this country. A great many were formerly slaves. On account of slavery the colored people are very generally poor and uneducated. Probably they are not yet capable of learning as fast and as much as white persons, or if they are, they have not had a good opportunity. They are willing to work, but need to be told what to do. They are not as ingenious or as prudent and thrifty as some white persons. Most of them are proud of their liberty and new right of voting, and seem endeavoring to improve. In some places the white people oppress or cheat them. But the law now declares that they shall everywhere have equal rights with white persons.

A gentleman riding in the cars by the side of a very intelligent-looking old colored man, asked him, "Why do not the negroes grow rich?" "Dey ain't savin'," he answered; "if dey gits a few dollars dey moves roun' a sight spryer to spen' it dan dey did to airn it.'' "Tell me," said the gentleman, "about the quarrels." Said the old negro, "Sometimes de white folks has a row, and sometimes de niggers has a row; sometimes de white folks pitches into de niggers, and sometimes de niggers pitches into de white folks — and den' agin dey don't. But I say, massa, *We wotes !*"

For colored people to call themselves "niggers" may not be amiss. For white persons to do so is vulgar and unkind.

The chief classes of people in America are the white people who were born here, the negroes, the Indians, and the immigrants. Of Indians there are about three hundred thousand. There is, however, very little chance of seeing one on a journey from Boston to Washington, for very few of them live in the towns and cities of Eastern States. When the discoverers first arrived in America, they did not know they had landed on a new continent, but supposed they had reached India. Therefore they called the copper-colored natives Indians. They soon found that the name was not a correct one, yet they continued to use it. Persons who wish to speak very accurately call the red men the aborigines.

"Aborigines" means "here from the beginning." There are numerous tribes of these American Indians, and they differ in character and habits. Some tribes are comparatively gentle, teachable, industrious and honest, and have become quite civilized. Others are fierce, wild, savage and treacherous. Some tribes live quietly on large tracts of land called Indian reservations, which have been set apart for them by government. Others roam over unsettled parts of the country, hunting and fishing as they find opportunity. And a small number dwell among the whites in the towns and villages. Most persons think that injustice has often been done to the Indians. It was when the great civil war was closing, and just before he was shot, that President Lincoln wrote, "I will not rest until they shall have justice."

A great many of our people came from foreign lands. Persons who *go* from a country to live in another are called emigrants. Persons who *come* from another country are called immigrants. Ever since America began to be settled, immigrants have been coming very steadily. As fast as they have found homes and work, many of them have written to their friends in the Old World, praising America and advising them to come. For three or four years past an immense number have been coming; in 1879 nearly 150,000; in 1880 more than 300,000; in 1881 probably 500,000. This is what made President Hayes say, "We see people coming, coming." They come from almost all European countries. Most of them are honest, industrious people, bring some money with them, and are anxious to buy farms, or to take work for wages as soon as possible. All such immigrants have always been made welcome. There is a curious office at Castle Garden, in New York City, where the shiploads of immigrants are received, and where they stay for a few days, until they can decide where to go. Officers are there ready to aid them. They need help, for they have not much education or business experience, and many of them do not understand our language.

America has for many years declared that every person who chose to leave his native land and remove to America or any other country had the right to do so. Many of the countries abroad have said,

" Our subjects have no right to move away without our leave." Great Britain used to say this; but in 1870 she made an agreement with our nation that the people of the two countries might come and go as they pleased. There is a somewhat similar agreement between China and the United States. Not quite a year ago Switzerland made a new law saying that poor persons not able to work, and young children, should not emigrate from Switzerland to America, unless there were friends or money here to support them. This law also says that the ships must carry Swiss emigrants comfortably, give them good food, and medicines if they are sick, and take good care of their baggage.

When an immigrant arrives, the law will immediately take care of him as a person. If any one cheats him, or steals from him, or hurts him, he can complain to the courts, just as if he were an American; and the wrong-doer will be punished. The immigrants have the benefit of our laws from their arrival. But a foreigner must be naturalized before he is allowed to vote. Naturalizing means that a court gives him leave to become a citizen. And he cannot be naturalized until he has lived in this country at least five years.

Of course young citizens will wish to know somewhat of the rules about children. The law means to be especially kind to children, and very careful and considerate of their welfare. Just as General Garfield said that his children should not be compelled to study until they were at least seven years old, so the judges all say, " We will not punish a child for anything, whatever it may do, before it is seven. Until then let its parents and teachers punish it if necessary." The law will protect the rights of the very youngest child. Any one who is cruel to a child, however young, may be punished. The littlest boy or girl may own property, and the judges will appoint a guardian to take care of it until the little owner grows old enough. Between seven and fourteen a child may be punished for breaking the laws, provided it knew better. If a policeman should arrest a grown man for stealing, and carry him before a judge to be punished, and the man should say that he did not know that stealing was against the law, the judge would say, "That makes no difference."

If the person arrested were a lad above seven but under fourteen, the judge would ask, " How do you know that this boy knew that what he did was wrong? Unless he knew that, I cannot send him to jail. His parents must take charge of him, or he should be sent to a school or society to be taught."

About a year ago a boy eleven years old was tried for assisting his father in killing a person. The judges said that as he was not fourteen, he could not be punished without proof that he knew the wrongfulness of what he did. Without this they would suppose that he was a dull, weak boy who did whatever he was told ; and they set him free. If the person arrested were a child under seven, the judge would not hear the complaint at all, except, perhaps, enough to send the little thing to some kind persons who would care for it. But in some of the States the laws state these ages somewhat differently.

It is often said until a lad is one and twenty he cannot make agreements. This is not quite correct. He cannot *bind himself* by his agreements. For example, it is not against the law for him to buy a horse, if any person will sell him one, nor for him to promise to pay the price next month, or next year. But the horse-dealer cannot compel the lad to pay the money by a lawsuit. If he should bring such a suit the judges would say, "This lad's promise to pay did not bind him, because he was not of age when he made it." The rule protects young persons from being cheated. They have twenty-one years allowed them for learning about business and property; and during those years they are not compelled to perform their bargains. Hence, whenever they find they have been cheated, they can "back out." This does not apply to marrying, though that is a kind of bargain. If a boy above fourteen or a girl above twelve were to be married, perhaps the law would say, "You cannot retract."

At twenty-one, the young man becomes "of age;" after that, his bargains are binding upon him. Whatever wages he earns belong to him, and he is allowed to vote. The same is true as to girls, except that they do not vote, and that, in one or two of the States, girls are called "of age" at eighteen.

In most European countries children have less liberty than in America. Thus in France there are

very stringent rules for keeping records of births ;
also a formal way of adopting a child, or of emanci-
pating one — that is, of setting him free from authority of his parents before he becomes of age. French
parents can by law govern their children more strictly,
and longer, than do Americans, and have much more
power to prevent their marrying; and can have a disobedient child, if under sixteen, imprisoned for a
month; one above sixteen, for six months, or even
more if six should not be enough. And if any one
else has left property to a child, the father can spend
the whole income, being only bound to maintain the
child suitably.

V.—THE RIDE TO NEW YORK.

"Nothing more aptly describes the character of our Republic than the solar system. . . The sun holds in the grasp of its attractive power the whole system, and imparts its light and heat to all, yet each individual planet is under the sway of laws peculiar to itself. . . So the States move on in their orbits of duty and obedience, bound to the central government by this constitution, which is their supreme law; while each State is making laws and regulations of its own, developing its own energies, maintaining its own industries, managing its local affairs in its own way."—GARFIELD: *Chips from the White House*, p. 422.

THE Travelling Law-school is now to ride in the cars from Boston to New York. We will notice on the way whether things which we see are under State law or under national. In the little villages almost the only national thing is the post-office. It is the United States government which carries all the letters and newspapers, owns all the mail-bags, employs all the postmasters and carriers; and it needs a great many post-offices. In New York the post-office is an immense stone edifice. On Western prairies the post-office is sometimes only a box upon a tall post. The carrier leaves the letters in the box, and the settlers look into the box, whenever convenient, for their letters.

Thus we can never tell by the size or importance of the building whether the business done within it is State or national. In Worcester, through which we pass, is a large and handsome asylum for insane persons. This, like most asylums, is under State laws. The next large city we pass is Springfield. Here is an armory. It is an immense establishment for manufacturing cannon, rifles, pistols, cartridges, and various equipments for the army. This armory is under United States laws. For whatever relates to the army is managed by the national government. A State does not have an army; if enemies come, and she needs one for driving them away, the Governor writes to the President, and the President orders a troop of soldiers of the national army to go and help that Governor and his State. The States have what is called the militia, or the national guard. The men between eighteen and forty-five are in duty bound to serve their State as soldiers, when needed, and they form companies and practise military evolutions, and learn how to load and fire. Whenever there is a war, and the nation needs a larger army than the national government has, the President asks the governors to send some of the militia. And the militia march forth from the States, and join the army, serving as soldiers under the President's orders while they are needed. This seems very perplexing. If the Governor needs the army, he must send to the President; and if the President lacks soldiers, he , must send to the Governor. But it hinders either government in making war upon the other. And military service is made very easy and inexpensive. In America the army is very small — only about twenty-five thousand men. It does not cost the people much, and whenever the people think it costs too much they can vote to make it smaller. They need not serve in the militia more than they vote to do.

All this is very different in foreign countries. In some, every young man must serve in the army for a few years, whether he wishes or not. In others, lots are drawn in all the villages once a year; and the lads who draw unlucky numbers are marched away to become soldiers. This is called the conscription.

Many interesting stories have been written about youths drawn in the French conscription. We never need a conscription, unless for a very short time when there is a great war. Never but once has there been a war in this country requiring a conscription, or a "draft," as it was called. The reason is, that all the States are united under one national government. And as long as that government can be maintained, no wars can arise between the States, and the army need not be very large. In Europe, the governments are independent, and therefore in more danger of war. So they need larger armies, and must have harsh laws for obtaining soldiers.

Switzerland is a small territory. It is defended by rivers and mountains against attacks from neighboring powers, and has an excellent government to preserve order in its own territory, and for these reasons has less need of an army; but every man has to be a soldier, and is drilled and assigned to a company. In time of peace the Swiss men engage in various kinds of business, but all have to be ready, in case either of the dangerous neighbors should make an attack, to join the army.

The navy, like the army, is under United States
laws, and may be quite small. At present the
American navy has about ninety steam vessels and
twenty-three sail vessels. This is a very small
number for so large a nation. Most of these were
hurriedly built during the civil war, and are nearly
worn out; for when a ship in the navy is fourteen
years old — just the age when a boy can be useful —
she is considered too old for important service.
Of the steam vessels in our navy, twenty-four are of
iron, sixty-six of wood. European countries have
built many iron and steel ships, much stronger than
any we Americans have; and many persons think
our navy ought to be made larger. Others think
the people should not be taxed for these costly
ships. As our governments are arranged, the States
are not at any expense for a navy, and the United
States need not spend any more for one than the
representatives of the people think best.

Soon after we pass Springfield, in our ride, we
shall cross the boundary line between New-York and
Connecticut. Shall we watch for the line? There
is nothing to be seen. A girl about twelve years old

was one day riding with her parents, and heard
her father say to her mother, "We are drawing
near the boundary between the two States." This
girl had studied geography, and knew about the
boundaries, and she thought she should like to see
one. So for a long time she sat looking out of the
window watching for it. At last she asked, " Papa,
when shall we come to the boundary line?"

"Oh, we have passed it."

"No, papa; I have watched carefully."

"Why, did you think there was a line you could
see, like a clothesline, or a telegraph line?"

"I thought there would be a line like the one
drawn on the maps."

"Oh, no," said her papa; "there is no actual
line. There is nothing to be seen. It is only the
place which men have agreed shall be called the end
of Massachusetts and the beginning of Connecticut.
Men can determine where it is by measuring, and
can put stakes to mark the place; but the real
boundary is an invisible thing. It is like the end of
an hour; people know when they come to it by the
hands of the clock, or hearing it strike; but the real

end of the hour cannot be seen or heard."

The girl thought this was difficult to understand, and it is. Yet the boundaries of the States are very important things.

About a hundred years ago there were but thirteen States; yet even then wise men saw that it would be best to form a Union or Federal government. Also, there was a great deal of wild land outside the thirteen States, and gradually enough persons settled upon various parts of it to form additional States, and these new States joined the Union. While a region of country is gradually growing thickly settled enough to become a State it is called a Territory; but it has a government very much like that of a State. At present there are thirty-eight States and eight such Territories.

Have you ever examined the American flag? There are thirteen horizontal stripes, red and white alternately: these represent the States which at first formed the Union. And there is a blue field in an upper corner, in which are now thirty-eight stars: these represent the whole number of States at the time when the flag was made. If you buy a flag,

count the stars and see if there are thirty-eight. If
not, the store-keeper is trying to sell you an old-fashioned flag. And whenever a new State is admitted
all flag-makers ought afterwards to work an additional star in their flags to represent it. The union
of the States is also expressed in the motto, *E plu-
ribus unum :* one from many. Americans have one
government, the Union, composed of many States.

One great benefit arising from the Union is that
there are no custom-houses at State boundaries, nor
are any passports required. Americans who go to
Europe learn that they must before starting get a
passport — which is a writing showing that the traveller is an American citizen. In crossing the boundaries of the various kingdoms and principalities
of the Continent, they often are required to show
their passports, and allow officers of the kingdoms
they are entering to examine their baggage. This
is very inconvenient. Few persons realize that if
it were not for the Union, travellers might probably
be required to exhibit passports and pay duties
at the custom-house — which is an office for collecting money to support the government — every

time they crossed a State boundary line. On the
journey the Travelling Law-school is taking this
would happen six times : first at the boundary of
Connecticut, again at the boundary of New York,
again on entering Jersey City, and on crossing into
Pennsylvania, Delaware and Maryland, one after
another.   It is the Union which saves us this annoy-
ance.

VI.—RAILROAD TRAVEL.

"The railroad has not only brought our people and their industries together, but it has carried civilization into the wilderness; has built up States and Territories which, but for its power, would have remained deserts for a century to come."—GARFIELD: *Chips from the White House*, p. 433.

THE ride of the Travelling Law-school from New Haven to New York will give an opportunity of explaining how to travel. Last fall a Mrs. Herman died in Germany, leaving two little children, Gottlieb and Frederika. Their father had come to this country a short time before, and they wished to follow him, but there was no grown person to bring them. Their friends bought tickets for them and put them on board a steamship and the brother took care of himself and his sister all the way, though he was only six years old and she but four and a half. The steamship people said that he behaved splendidly. When they reached Castle Garden, which is a sort of hotel for immigrants in New York City, the superintendent put them in a car to ride to their father's home somewhere in Illinois. As the conductor and brakemen would help and watch over them, they probably made the long trip safely. Thus we see that very young people may need to take long journeys. Travelling is perplexing at first, but becomes easy and pleasant when one understands it.

If any one wishes to know which government has most control of travel, the answer is that conveyances by water are governed by the United States, but journeying on land is chiefly subject to the State in which the traveller is. Some persons think it would be better for the United States to make all the laws respecting journeys from one State to another, so that the laws should be uniform; but this has not yet been done. Travellers, however, are not much concerned with these great laws. They have more need to know the rules made by the companies, and the customs of travellers. These customs or usages are not exactly laws, yet it is wise to follow them; for if two persons ask a court to decide a dispute, and the judge finds there is no distinct law to settle it, he

will inquire, "What is customary in such cases?"
A court often treats usages of the people as forming
a sort of law, if they are reasonable, convenient, and
widely known. Law questions about travelling are
often decided according to the usages of travellers.
The best way of learning these usages is to watch
what older travellers do, or to ask them what is customary. The companies must give notice of their
regulations. There are various ways, as by posting
a placard in the depot or car, printing the rule on
the tickets, or stationing a gateman to tell passengers as they pass him what they must do.

It is important to know that the conductor is what
may be called the "captain" of the train. He controls everything on the journey except the management of the engine. The ticket-seller and the baggage-man do not go on the cars, they remain at the
depot, and renew their services to the next train.
The engineer, with a fireman or two to aid him, manages the engine, and the passengers scarcely see him.
The brakemen do whatever the conductor directs,
and will answer any civil questions which a passenger
needs to put. The whole authority, as far as passen-

gers are concerned, is in the conductor. He is the
person to explain the regulations, and to enforce them
if a passenger, after being told, will not obey.

When a gentleman having a lady in his charge
reaches the station to take passage in the cars, it is
usually best for him to leave the trunks in some
one's care and to escort the lady to the Ladies'
room, where she may sit while he makes the arrangements. There will probably be two rooms, one
labelled LADIES' ROOM, another GENTLEMEN'S ROOM.
These signs are a regulation of the company that
ladies are to have the use of one and men travelling
alone are to occupy the other; but a gentleman travelling with a lady can sit with her in the Ladies'
room. In a large depot there will be many other
doors with signs upon them, such as "DINING
ROOM;" "SUPERINTENDENT'S ROOM;" "OUTWARD
BAGGAGE ROOM." These signs are regulations to in-
form passengers whether they may enter the rooms
or not. If one wishes to obey the rules, it is easy to
judge by the sign over a door whether he may go in
or not; and he may almost always be sure that a door
with no sign is not for passengers. If one is "prowl-

ing around," like Bluebeard's wife, full of curiosity to go into rooms where he is not wanted, the signs will not hinder him. But the companies have the right, by law, to set apart some rooms where passengers must not go, and one who disobeys the sign and goes in may be ordered out, and even expelled by force. A person who makes noise or disturbance in the passengers' room, or smokes where the rule " No Smoking " is posted, may be expelled.

The next thing for the gentleman to do is to buy tickets. There is almost sure to be a sign " Ticket-office." This is a regulation that whoever wishes to ride should not trust to paying fare to the conductor, but must buy a ticket beforehand. If, indeed, a conductor should find a passenger riding who had no ticket, but was willing to pay, he would take the money ; he would not put the passenger off the car. But he would charge a little extra. The fare thus paid is usually five or ten cents more than the cost of a ticket. This is to make passengers careful to buy tickets. There is usually a ticket-window for ladies, opening into the Ladies' room. It is better to buy tickets before going to check the baggage, because there may be a regulation of the company — there is one in many large depots — that the baggage-master must not give checks for trunks until the tickets are shown to him. Where there is such a regulation, a passenger who goes first to check baggage will be sent back to buy a ticket. An experienced traveller will take notice whether there is a " queue " in front of the ticket-office, and if there is one, he will take his place in the line behind the last man, and move slowly up until he reaches the window in his turn. Ask some grown person to describe a queue to you. There is very seldom any need to form a queue at a railroad ticket-office : on a steamboat one is almost always formed. If a person should disregard the queue and walk up to the window at one side, the ticket-seller would tell him to stand back, and the other passengers would grumble, " Take your turn." If he persisted and made trouble he could be arrested and taken to court; and the judge would say, " You are fined for disorderly conduct. It is the usage of travellers to form a queue for buying tickets whenever there is a crowd; and persons who take journeys should learn such usages and conform to them."

The next thing in order is to get checks for the trunks. Most passengers have some small articles which they carry with them, and also a trunk, which the hackman, when he brings the party to the depot, leaves with the baggage-master. When the passenger comes he points out his trunk and tells the baggage-master whither he is going, and the baggage-master gives him a queer little bit of brass having a number and some mysterious letters stamped upon it. This is the check. If you watch a baggage-man when he gives a check you will see that he has another similar bit of brass which hangs at the end of a strap, and by this strap he will fasten this bit to the handle of the trunk. If you can compare the two you will see that the stamped numbers are the same. The shape of the check, and the letters show the baggage-men all along the road at which station the trunk is to be put off; and the number shows that it belongs to the passenger who produces, at the stopping-place, the check with the corresponding number. Baggage-men have to be very careful to keep the checks separately, for if they become mixed the trunks will go astray all over the country. And a passenger needs to keep his check carefully, for if a dishonest person should steal or find it, he, instead of the owner, can get the trunk.

The next question is about going aboard the cars. Perhaps a gong or bell will strike to let passengers know when the car is ready. There may be a gateman who will say, as the passengers pass him, "Show your tickets." This is a regulation which one must obey. You will almost always at way stations find a time-table posted in the passengers' room. This is a regulation prescribed by the company to govern the running of trains. The conductor and the engineer have copies of the time-table, and if they find the train is reaching the station a little ahead of time they run somewhat slower. Oftener they get behind time, and then they run faster and try to make up; but sometimes they cannot do so. In studying a time-table, remember that the time of day is a little different in different towns and cities. If the watches of the Travelling Law-school were just right by the best clock in Boston, they will be nearly fifteen minutes slow when we reach New York. Owing to this, a person may find that his train arrives sooner or later than he expected, judging by his own watch, and yet the train may be on time, judged by railroad time. In all close calculations be sure you have railroad time.

When you go to the train you will perhaps find there is a ladies' car, or a drawing-room car, but there is always a brakeman or porter ready to tell passengers about these. In ordinary cars passengers are supposed to know the rules and usages without being told. It is not wrong for one person to take the whole of the double seat, or for two persons to turn one seat over so as to face backwards, and occupy the two, if there are plenty of seats for other passengers. But no one has a right to keep more than one seat if there be any passenger who lacks a seat; when any person does this it is proper to appeal to the conductor, and he will compel the uncivil passenger to give up the extra place. Every experienced and considerate traveller watches as the car fills, and when he sees that the seats are nearly all taken he empties the extra seat so that it shall be ready for the next comer.

A very important usage of travel is that one can

keep a seat by leaving an article of baggage in it. Whenever, therefore, on entering the car, you find that many seats have overcoats or valises or umbrellas in them, it is best to consider them as taken, and look for others. If an ignorant passenger should dump such a valise in the alley-way of the car and take the seat himself, the owner would before long return and claim the seat. If the ignorant passenger refused to leave it, the owner of the valise could, if he chose, appeal to the conductor, and the conductor would probably say that he was entitled to it. If the ignorant passenger would not yield, the conductor could call a brakeman, and they two would have the right to pull him out by force, and even, if he continued to make trouble, to stop the train and put him off. Conductors are usually very unwilling to do these things, but they have authority to expel passengers who disobey the rules or will not pay fare from the cars.

VII.—IN NEW YORK AND AROUND IT.

"As an abstract theory, the doctrine of free trade seems to be universally true; but as a question of practicability, under a government like ours, the protective system seems to be indispensable. . . I am for a protection that leads to ultimate free trade."—GARFIELD: *Chips from the White House*, pp. 392, 407.

ALTHOUGH New York City is the largest city in the State, it is not the capital. Boston is the largest city in Massachusetts, and is also the capital; but not because it is so large. A city is sometimes called "metropolis," or "emporium," to signify that it is large and important; but it is not called the capital of the State unless it has been selected as the place for building the State House and doing the business of the State government. Remember that a capital city need not be a large one.

There are many interesting things in New York. There is a very large park, containing a pond for boating or skating, a music stand with a band to play

in summer afternoons, a curious cave and ramble,
several cosey summer-houses and refreshment-sa-
loons, many wonderful birds and beasts, and some
trained ponies and carriages drawn by goats for
children. There are broad and handsome streets,
some lined with elegant dwellings, others with
shops exhibiting curious and beautiful things for
sale. There are large and costly churches, libraries,
school-houses, banks, hotels, museums and theatres,
also what are called elevated railroads, which are
built upon posts so that the cars run upon a level with
the second or third stories of houses, while other cars
and ordinary carts and carriages run underneath
them. The chief street for business is Broadway, the
sidewalks of which are thronged with people walking,
while the street itself is so crowded with vehicles that
sometimes they cannot move, but have to wait until
the policemen can untangle the "jam." If we should
go to the crowded end of Broadway and watch a lady
out a-shopping who wished to cross the street, we
should see her standing at the corner looking very
anxiously among the stages and carts. Soon a
policeman would approach and say, "Do you wish

to cross, madam?" She would say, "Yes." Then
he would "arrest" her by one arm, very politely, and
walk with her right in among the carriages. At first
she would be a little "scared;" but he would shake
his club on this side or that at the horses or their
drivers, and they would stop or turn aside, and thus
in a minute the lady would be safely across. Then
she would turn half way around and say with a smile,
"Thank you, sir." By this you would see that
what the teacher told you in December is true —
a chief duty of policemen is to help people out of
difficulty. And no honest, well-behaved person need
be afraid of them. Whenever you are in trouble
in a city street, it is well to ask aid from a policeman.

New York has grown thus large and wealthy by
reason of her spacious harbor and fine accommoda-
tions for ships which bring goods from foreign lands
to America. All little citizens know that the things
people eat and drink or wear or use for furnishing
their houses come from different parts of the world.
One region has the best soil and climate for producing
wheat, another for beef, another for cotton, another

for tea or coffee, another for coal, iron or gold. Also, the various nations have different taste and skill about making things; thus some can manufacture silks or shawls better than anything else; others prefer to make woollen or cotton cloth, or crockery, or iron ware. Of course the dwellers in each region like to exchange what they can raise or manufacture, and therefore have in great plenty, for what they cannot produce. This exchanging of goods between different parts of the world is called "commerce," and the persons who attend particularly to it are "merchants." Foreign commerce needs good harbors; and New York supplies one. The city occupies a long, narrow island, on each side of which is a broad space of still and sheltered water called New York bay, which, toward the south, opens to the Atlantic Ocean through a strait called the Narrows; this is of just the proper width to admit ships from Europe, while it keeps out the ocean storms. The shore of the island on each side is well adapted for wharves and piers at which these vessels can exchange cargoes. West of the island is a large river called Hudson or North river, up which vessels can sail fully a hundred miles carrying goods to the northern part of the country. If we were to sail up this river all night in a steamboat we should land in the morning at the capital city — Albany. At Albany commences a canal along which goods can be carried to the West. For carrying goods from New York to the East there is a curious strip of water called East river; and vessels for southern ports can sail down through the Narrows and along the Atlantic coast. Besides these water-ways there are great railroads branching from New York to all parts of the country. If you will ask some grown person to explain this on a map you will see very clearly that New York is an excellent port for foreign commerce.

Foreign commerce is one of the things placed under the charge of the United States government. Each State governs any commerce there may be within our own limits, but commerce among the States is subject only to the government at Washington. All persons who "import" goods, that is, bring them into this country for sale, are required to pay some money for the privilege of doing so. This money is called the "duty," and is collected at the custom-house in the port where the vessel arrives; in New York the custom-house is an immense building, and several hundred officers, clerks, brokers and messengers are kept busy in ascertaining and collecting the duties on the various cargoes which arrive in the harbor from foreign lands. The government at Washington has published a list of goods likely to be imported, specifying what duty must be paid upon each; this is called the tariff. Suppose a merchant imports a cargo of tea from China. When the ship arrives, an officer from the custom-house visits her, counts and weighs the boxes, and ascertains the quality and value of the tea; he then consults the tariff to see what duty is charged upon such tea, and computes what sum must be paid for allowing the cargo to enter. He notifies the merchant. The latter pays the duty at the custom-house, and the money is sent to Washington, where it is used to support the government. And the custom-house officers allow the tea to be brought ashore and unpacked for sale. If a merchant should refuse to pay the duty, he would not be allowed to bring his goods ashore. Sometimes persons contrive to brings goods

secretly, without paying duty; this is called "smuggling," and is a serious offence.   Passengers coming
from Europe sometimes endeavor to smuggle goods;
it is to prevent this that custom-house officers search
their baggage.   Some of the tricks of smugglers are
very ingenious.   A lady once landed from a steamer
leading a shaggy yellow dog; but the dog was so
fat and waddled so clumsily that the custom-house
officers suspected smuggling.   They caught the dog
and cut into his skin.   Under the skin they found a
great many yards of costly lace wound around the
body of a lean, lank black-and-tan terrier.   The outside skin was the skin of some other dog which had
been sewed over the lace in hope of smuggling
the lace.

Every importing merchant must of course add the
amount of the duty paid upon his goods to the price
he asks for them.   If a piece of cloth a hundred
yards long costs in France $50, and the expense of
the voyage is $10 per piece, and a fair profit for the
merchant is $15, then, in case there is no duty, the
merchant can sell the cloth at seventy-five cents per
yard; but if the duty is twenty-five cents he must

raise his price to $1. This will hinder the people
from buying it, and make them more willing to buy
cloth made in America instead. It has always been
a perplexing question whether it is better that government should charge high duties on foreign goods,
and thus "protect" manufacturers in this country
against the competition of those foreign lands, or
allow the people to buy whatever is cheapest wherever
they please. Laying high duties to prevent foreign
competition is called "protection," and is better
for manufacturers and producers. Laying no duties
(or very low ones) is called "free trade," and is better
for merchants and ship-owners. If a father of five
children should give them a dollar apiece to expend
in Christmas presents, and should say, "I advise
you to visit all the shops, and consider carefully
where you can buy presents cheapest," this would be
like entire free trade. But if, instead, he should
say, "I do not wish you to spend this money in the
shops, but among each other; let each child make
the best gifts he or she can — boats, sleds, boxes, book-
marks, pin-cushions, slippers — and each buy from
the others," this would be like complete protection.

By the free-trade plan the children would undoubtedly get the handsomest gifts for the money. By the protection plan, they would keep the money among them, and would also gain excellent practice in making fancy articles. Which is the best plan? Perhaps you will agree with General Garfield's opinion, which is our motto. In this country we never have either free trade or protection entire or complete. At present we have partial or moderate protection; people can import foreign goods, notwithstanding they are such as could be procured here, if they are willing to pay a duty on them.

VIII.—BARGAINS AND BUSINESS.

"Confidence in promises lawfully made is the life-blood of trade and commerce. It is the vital air labor breathes. It is the light which shines in the pathway of prosperity."—GARFIELD: *Chips from the White-House*, p. 443.

WHAT does the Travelling Law-School wish to study while beginning the ride from New York to Philadelphia? How to succeed in business."

"Yes; and how to make good bargains."

Excellent. There are probably a thousand books explaining the law about bargains and business; and lawyers who study them become very much interested in the various rules. But it is quite possible for young persons to begin business, and to prosper in it, without having learned much about the law. The chief object of having laws is to make people who are not honest, industrious, faithful, sensible and courteous, behave somewhat as if they were so. Hence, whoever has these qualities naturally, and makes bargains, or does business with good people, will very seldom have any trouble about the law. Good qualities of character, and good friends and acquaintances, are a young person's best assurance of succeeding in bargains and business.

Some excellent business qualities are, however, quite opposite to each other. If one could choose his own traits, it would be a perplexing question as to some, which to choose.

Ingenuity or docility. The question is perplexing whether a young person beginning business will succeed best by doing exactly as he is told without asking questions — which is called docility — or by using ingenuity in making improvements.

A poor man once asked the rich Mr. Girard for work; and Mr. Girard said, "You see tem stone yondare?"

"Yes, sir," said the man.

"Vare well; you shall bring tem, and pile tem here."

The man worked till noon doing so, and then told

Mr. Girard that the job was done, and asked what he should do next.

"Ah, ha! Oui! you shall go place tem stone where you got him."

Mr. Girard did not really care where the stones lay — he was only trying the workman.

At night the man reported that he had carried the stones all back; and Mr. Girard paid him a dollar. Next day the man had the same task given him — of moving the stones back and forth — and did it as before.

"Ah!" said Mr. Girard at night, "you shall be my man; you mind your own business and do it; you ask no questions." And the poor man thus obtained an excellent position.

Many employers wish their "hands" to do just as they are told. It is an excellent quality, if one is not stupid. A lad once went to learn shoemaking, and the master gave him some leather, and a knife and pattern, and told him to cut out pieces of the leather exactly like the pattern. Now the pattern had a hole in it cut for hanging it on a nail; and the poor boy, meaning to do just as he was told, cut a similar hole in all his pieces. This spoiled them, and the master dismissed him; which seems unjust. One needs, however, to use common sense even in obeying orders. And sometimes persons have succeeded wonderfully by ingenuity in doing better than they were told. When steam-engines were first invented, it was common to employ some one to open and shut a certain valve. A boy who was employed to do this took notice that a particular crank or lever in the machinery moved regularly just at the moment for opening the valve; and he contrived, with a piece of cord, to tie the handle of the valve to this moving part of the machinery, after which the engine itself opened and shut the valve. When the employer saw this he was greatly pleased, for the contrivance led to a great improvement in the steam-engine.

Ingenuity like this is a natural gift. Those boys and girls who really have it are very fortunate. But unless one has remarkable ingenuity, doing exactly as he is told, or as he sees other people do, is the best. He then does not need much knowledge of law. An ingenious, reforming person needs more; for he may be breaking some law by his improvements, without knowing it. Also he needs to know the law about obtaining patents for his improvements when they are good.

Shrewdness or simplicity. A boy who lived near a mill observed that a long wooden pole in the machinery was wearing out. He knew, somehow, that it could not be replaced by a green tree; a seasoned stem would be needed whenever the old one broke. So he cut down a tree of the right size, hauled it to his father's dooryard, and let it lie there to dry and season. In about six months the mill-owner came rapping at the door.

"What will you take for that pole?" he asked.

"One hundred dollars," said the boy.

"A hundred dollars for that common pole?"

"Yes, sir; I saw your pole was wearing out, and I thought you would rather pay a good price than have the mill stopped while another was seasoning. So I got one ready for you." And the mill-owner found he had better pay the money.

This is an example of shrewdness. It is a natural gift, and persons who have it are very fortunate, provided they also have honesty. Years ago a boy

advertised that to every person sending him twenty-
five cents, he would mail a steel-plate portrait, fairly
executed, of the famous president, Andrew Jackson.
Whenever a letter with twenty-five cents came, he
immediately forwarded a two-cent postage stamp !
Of course people soon began to complain, and the
post-office authorities stopped the fraud.   This was a
shrewd plan, for when the contriver was arrested for
swindling, he could say, " I did exactly what I promised ; I did not promise a large portrait, but only
a fairly executed one."   But it was dishonest shrewdness.   One objection to shrewdness is, that often
where it is not perhaps really dishonest, it seems
dishonest to those who are not naturally shrewd.
Plain people are apt to suspect and dislike shrewd
ones.   Whether the mill-owner would be willing to
employ the boy who sold him the pole, in his mill,
would depend on the boy's being moderate in the
price he asked, and the man's being good-natured.
Many a man would feel what is called " overreached,"
and would be angry, even if he paid the money.
Still, honest shrewdness is an advantage.   But young
persons who have not that natural gift can succeed in

bargains and business by cultivating simple, straightforward, distinct ways. Perhaps you cannot make yourself uncommonly shrewd, but you can learn to be simple, clear and frank in your dealings. A youth who is candid in explaining what work he is willing to do; who says distinctly what wages he thinks he ought to have; who makes a memorandum of the bargain, or preserves the letters which were written about the business; who does as he promises; who keeps accurate accounts of what he earns and receives, and who saves part of his earnings on interest, is more likely to succeed than if he were remarkably shrewd but had not learned these things. He is not trying to get advantage over other people, but to help them, hence they are not suspicious or jealous of him, but are willing to help him. His plain common sense, and his frank, distinct way of explaining what he means, aid him to avoid misunderstandings; and when a dispute arises, it is easily settled without a law-suit. But a person gifted with shrewdness needs to study the law carefully to know just how far he may go in making his shrewd bargains.

Versatility or perseverance. By versatility is meant the gift which some people have of doing a great many kinds of work, and of changing their plans readily when circumstances change. A young man was once making his first speech in the House of Commons, but he was not a good speaker, and the members laughed at him and would not listen. At last he stopped, shouting, " I shall sit down now, but the time will come when you shall hear me." He then persisted in studying and practising, and became a very skilful orator in that very house, and was, at length, the famous Lord Beaconsfield. Every one now properly praises his persistence.

Once when commerce had lately been opened with a certain hot country, a London merchant sent thither a cargo of warming-pans. Now warming-pans were useless in so warm a climate, and everybody laughed, — no one would buy. There was, however, a great deal of sugar-making there ; and the merchant ordered his agent to take off the covers and advertise the warming-pans as sugar-ladles ! They were just what were convenient for dipping the hot cane-juice out of the boilers, and they sold at a great profit.

This was a very judicious change of plan. If the merchant had persisted in his warming-pan project he would have lost his money. To know when to persist and when to change is very difficult.

Some persons succeed in doing several kinds of business, and in making and performing a great variety of bargains, together. This versatility, however, is a rare gift. Most young persons will succeed best by adhering to one plan, steadily; making changes only when there are very strong reasons for doing so. Those who adopt this course will find that their business will run along smoothly without many law-suits. Persons gifted with versatility, whenever they start a new enterprise, should study new law corresponding to it.

If there were more time we would discuss whether it is best to be enterprising or prudent; to be liberal or economical; to be courteous or summary; and some other like riddles. But we must see what we pass on the way to Philadelphia.

IX.— TO PHILADELPHIA, AND WHAT WE SEE THERE.

> " Let us have equality of dollars before the law, so that the trinity of our political creed shall be, equal States, equal men, and equal dollars, throughout the Union." GARFIELD : *Chips from the White House*, page 454.

WHILE the Travelling Law-school have been talking about bargains and business, they have reached Newark. This place is famous for its manufacturing establishments. Here are made in great quantities, steam-engines, carriages, iron and tin ware, saddles, telegraphic instruments, rubber and celluloid articles, Russia leather, soap— in short, an endless variety of goods. It is said that a greater number of useful inventions have been produced by Newarkers than by the inhabitants of any other city in the land. You already know that importing is governed by the national government. Manufacturing is governed by the States; each State makes laws for whatever factories are within its limits. The reason is, that importing is bringing goods from abroad, manufacturing is done at home. Now it is the American plan to have a national government for taking care of foreign affairs, State governments for domestic affairs; thus the manufactories of Newark (and of Rahway, not far beyond) are subject to the laws of New Jersey, and the government at Washington has scarcely anything to say about them.' Soon we shall pass New Brunswick and Princeton, where are famous colleges. These, like factories, are governed more by State than by national laws. The colleges also make laws for the students. Just as people living in a town or city are expected to obey the laws of the corporation, and passengers in a railroad train must obey the company's regulations, so students in a college ought to obey the rules of the college.

In this country the students of a college and the people of the town where the college is built are, usually, independent of each other; the townspeople obey the town by-laws, and the students obey (or ought to obey) the college faculty; but in many foreign places it has come to pass that colleges have gained authority over the townspeople. This is partly because these colleges are so ancient and permanent. Thus the famous Oxford University, near London, is far older than any such institution in America. It is also larger and wealthier. Gradually it has acquired influence and authority over local affairs, until now it quite governs the town, instead of the town governing the University.

Harper's Magazine once published a composition written in the year 1700, by an Oxford school-boy, upon "tyrants." It reads thus :

A tyrant is a savage hideous beast. Imagine that you saw a certain monster armed on all sides with 500 horns on all sides dreadful fatnd with humane entrails, drunken with humane blood this is the fatal mischief whom they call a tyrant.

WILLIAM.

From reading this composition we may conclude that school-boys were about the same then as now, but that governments were more oppressive two centuries ago than in our day. American boys do not hear or care enough about tyrants to write compositions upon them, nor would they write such an exaggerated description.

Soon we shall pass Trenton. This is a capital city, the capital of New Jersey. Here, therefore, is a State House, and here we should generally find a governor, and, at the proper time of year, a legislature, just as in Boston.

Now we travel onward, passing another boundary line without seeing it, and at length draw into Philadelphia. This is not a capital city. It is the largest city in Pennsylvania, but Harrisburg is the capital. But it is a very attractive metropolis, containing many beautiful and important buildings, also a delightful park, called Fairmount, where, about six years ago, the famous World's Fair was held. A world's fair is partly a national, partly a State matter; thus the general government at Washington invited the foreign governments to send their manufacturers and workmen, but the State government at Harrisburg had most to say about the land and the buildings for the exhibition.

Philadelphia is a famous city in the history of our government. It was founded by William Penn, who set an excellent example of justice and kindness in dealing with the Indians inhabiting the land when he and his colony came.   Here Franklin lived when he was a printer's boy.   Here was written the Declaration of Independence ; here the congress of the colonies adopted it ; here it was brought forth and read to the assembled people, in the State House yard, on the Fourth of July, 1776.   And here Congress often met until Washington City was founded.

There is in Philadelphia a celebrated building called Independence Hall.   It was originally the State House, but now it is stored with curiosities connected with the history of the government.   It has been refitted to look as much as possible as it did in 1776.   It contains the ancient and quaint desk on which the Declaration was signed; the armchair of John Hancock ; the original draft of the Declaration, and the chairs and portraits of the signers.   There is also a National Museum, where a great many similar relics are preserved ; one of the most curious is the Independence Bell, which rang to proclaim the adoption of the Declaration and the birth of the new nation.   All these things are

very interesting for a Travelling Law-school to
see.

Another very important building is the United
States Mint. A mint is a kind of factory where
money — such as eagles, dollars, halves and quarters,
and dimes — are coined or manufactured. The whole
business of making gold and silver money is done by
the United States government; the States are not
allowed to make any, neither are towns, or cities, or
individuals. A reason for this is that if any one who
chose might manufacture money, there would soon
be so many kinds as to perplex the people. Therefore all coins are made by the Federal government.
If a person has gold or silver and wishes to have it
made into money, he must send it to a mint — there
are five mints in different parts of the country, but
that at Philadelphia is the most important — and ask
to have it coined. Coining is a very curious and
beautiful process. The object of it is to make sure
that the pieces shall contain exactly the right quantity
of the metal. When gold is cut into round pieces of
precisely the right size and weight, and pictures are
stamped on each side, and curious marks called

"milling" are pressed upon the edge, no person can take away any portion, however small, without detection; for wherever any is taken, a little of the picture or milling will be spoiled.

Only metallic money is made at mints; the bank-notes and treasury notes are printed at Washington. But these notes are not really money: they are only called so, because they are used instead of money. A bank-note is a promise by a bank to pay a certain sum. A treasury note or "greenback" is a promise by the United States government to pay the sum named. The reason why these paper promises can be used for money is that they are so much lighter and easier to carry, and that people generally understand they can get gold money for them whenever they wish. When a single bank becomes unable to pay money for its notes, people say that "the bank has failed;" and then its business is stopped. Sometimes all the banks and the government also have been unable to pay gold money—or "specie" as it is called—for their promises. Such a state of things makes a great deal of trouble; yet if people know that some day sufficient specie will be made, and the

promises will be paid, they can use the paper promises for a while as if they were really money.   But if
they did not expect that one day payment in specie
would be made, they would soon refuse to take the
paper promises for money, and the consequence
would be that the bank-notes and treasury-notes,
however prettily they were printed, would become
worthless, except as pictures.   It is of great importance that enough gold and silver money should
be made at the mints to make it certain that the
paper money all over the country can be paid in
specie whenever any one who holds it chooses specie.
This is what President Garfield meant by saying:
" Let us have equality of dollars."

X.—MONEY AND BANKS.

" The State Bank system was a chaos of ruin, in which the business of the country was again and again engulfed. The people rejoice that it has been swept away, and they will not consent to its re-establishment. In its place we have the National Bank System, based on the bonds of the United States, and sharing the safety and credit of the government "— GARFIELD: *Chips from the White House*, p. 420.

A BANK is a sort of a mill-pond for money. When a natural cascade is not strong enough for turning the mill-wheel, men build a dam, and collect the water which runs from a hundred springs and brooks above, and this water they let down whenever needed, through a gate and a flume, in a little torrent, upon the wheel. All over the land are men who have worked a good many years and saved their money, and now they wish to work less and have their money at interest; for they have more money than they need for their business. They are the springs and brooks from which money is running. There are other men who are young, industrious and enterprising; they have not so much money as their business needs, but can make more profits if some one will lend them money to build stores or factories, buy goods or materials, hire clerks or workmen. Their wheels need a flood to turn them. For this purpose of turning the wheels of business, a few men in some chief town join in forming a bank, to receive the money of those who have more than they are using, and loan it to those who need more than they have.

There are two ways in which money flows into a bank: "stock" and "deposits." When a bank is formed, each owner contributes such money as he wishes, one ten thousand dollars, another one thousand, another perhaps only five hundred. These sums, added together, form what is called the "capital" of the bank, which is used by the managers in conducting the business. Also business men of the neighborhood usually like to keep part of their money in the bank because it is a safer place than their stores and houses. A bank usually has solid vaults and strong fire-proof safes, for keeping money, and a part of its business is to receive money for people and keep it safely until the owners wish to spend it. The moneys which persons lodge in the bank to be kept for them are called the "deposits," because they are "deposited," that is, left for safe keeping. Whenever they wish to spend any of the money they have deposited, they write a "check," asking the bank to pay so much, and the bank does so. Meantime the capital and the deposits together make a large sum. A small portion must be kept in the drawers for doing business from day to day, but the larger part forms what we may call a mill-pond of money, ready to be loaned to men who need more than they have in their business.

The most common way of letting the money run from the bank's mill-pond upon the merchants' mill-wheels is called "discounting." Often the reason why a merchant needs money is because he has sold goods, but has had to take his pay in notes instead of cash. Ask some grown person to explain to you about taking notes. He does not wish, however, to wait for his money until the notes are paid, therefore he carries them to the bank and asks to have them discounted.

A man who has not any notes given him by his customers sometimes himself makes a note to be discounted. When a note is brought to a bank for discount, or if the bank has not money to spare, or if the officers are not sure the note will be paid, they say no. Banks have several curious ways, which there is not time to explain, of making sure that the notes they discount will be paid when the time comes. Let us suppose, however, that the officers are willing to discount the note, and that it reads:

> For value received, I promise to pay to John Smith, or order, one thousand dollars, in two months from date.
>
> THOMAS JOHNSON.

The officers will compute two months' interest on one thousand dollars. They learned how to do this from the arithmetic, at school. This ten dollars is the "discount," or the bank's profit, for letting Mr. Smith have the money. The bank lets him have nine hundred and ninety dollars out of its mill-pond; and Mr. Smith writes on the back of the note:

> Pay to the —— Bank, or order.
>
> JOHN SMITH.

and gives the note to the bank officers. The nine hundred and ninety dollars will soon drive the mill-wheel of Mr. Smith's business. When the two months are ended, the bank collects the one thousand dollars from Mr. Johnson, and thus gets back the nine hundred and ninety, with ten additional for "discount" or profit. The discounts or profits are kept together for six months or a year, and then are divided among the stockholders, to pay them for letting the bank have the "capital." If Mr. Johnson should not pay the note promptly, Mr. Smith would be required to pay it. This plan of buying merchants' notes at a small profit is called "discounting," and is a large part of a bank's business.

Whether obtaining discounts is wise or not depends on circumstances. Often it is foolish ; merchants frequently fail because they have had their notes discounted and have given a considerable part to the banks and spent the rest unwisely, when, if they had kept the notes and collected them when they became due, they would have had the whole of the money. And banks sometimes fail because the officers are imprudent or dishonest. But there is no doubt it is

a good plan to have banks in operation, so that a prudent merchant can obtain discounts when it is really
best to do so.   If there were no banks, a great many
people would have to keep their savings in old stock-
ings, or bureau drawers, or boxes buried in the ground,
could get no interest upon it, and very likely it would
be stolen; and on the other hand, many merchants
would be unable to do business for want of the use
of that very money. Banks are excellent things, though
they need to be managed honestly, and used prudently.

When a bank is formed, the stockholders, or men
who contribute the capital, elect a few "directors" to
direct how the business shall be done.   These directors elect a "president," who usually attends at the
bank daily to superintend or preside over the management.   They also choose a "cashier," who takes
care of the notes that are discounted, talks with the
customers, writes letters, oversees the accounts and
instructs the various clerks in their duties.   There are
also a "teller" to receive the deposits and to pay the
checks; a "bookkeeper" to keep accounts; and
a "porter" to go of errands, and lock the banking-
house at night.   Large banks in the cities have two

tellers, one to pay the checks written by persons who
have deposited money in the bank, asking for some of
it—he is called the paying, or first teller; and one to
receive the deposits, called the receiving or second
teller; also two or three bookkeepers and clerks,
such as a " discount clerk " to keep a list of the notes
discounted; also several messengers. A place as
" bank messenger " is an excellent one for a boy who
is honest, pleasant, industrious, frugal, and shrewd
about money; for he has a good opportunity to grow
up in the bank, and be chosen assistant bookkeeper,
book-keeper, second teller, first teller and cashier in
turn, and even president if he is successful in saving
money enough to buy shares of stock.

You will wish to know whether banks are under
State or national laws. Formerly nearly all banks
were under State laws. Some of the States governed
them very well, others not so well. About twenty years
ago the United States government decided to establish
some banks also; and now, when people in any place
wish to start a bank, they can do so under the law of the
State, or under the United States law, as they please.
Banks formed under the United States law are called

National Banks; you can always know them by their having the word "national" in the name. These banks have it for a part of their business to issue the bank notes which people use as money. A national bank deposits part of its capital in the Treasury department at Washington, and the Treasury department gives it, in return, a parcel of bank notes. It uses these notes in discounting notes for merchants, and in other business. Almost any grown person can show you a national-bank note. Whenever any one who has a national-bank note desires to do so he can present it to the officers of the bank and demand gold for the sum which the note promises to pay, and they must give it to him. If they will not, there are arrangements by which the note can be sent to Washington, and the gold for it will be paid there out of the capital which the bank deposited there on obtaining the notes. Thus the national-bank notes are perfectly safe. In the whole twenty years no person has ever lost money by failure of a national bank to pay its notes.

XI.—IN WASHINGTON CITY.

"Let any American who can, travel abroad, as I have done, and with the opportunity of witnessing what there is to be seen that I have had, and he will return to America a better American and a better citizen than when he went away. He will return more in love with his own country." —GRANT: *Chips from the White House,* p. 341.

THE Travelling Law-school has now reached Washington City; and, for the first time, is not in any State. We are in the District of Columbia. The wise men who formed the Federal Government feared that if they chose a city within some State to be the capital of the new nation, that State might endeavor to make laws governing what the national officers should do in its city; therefore a district was set apart which should not be in any State, but under the sole control of Congress; and in this district the capital city for the entire country, Washington, has been built. The rule which holds almost everywhere else, that there are three governments, national, State and municipal, does not apply in Washington; here are only two, the national and the city governments. Curiously, because the people of Washington are not in a State, they do not choose a representative in Congress, nor have they a senator, nor can they vote for President.

Washington City is remarkable for its broad and nicely paved streets, and for open parks and circles with ornamental fences and statues or monuments, and for magnificent public buildings. It has not so many fine stores as Boston, New York or Philadelphia. The most interesting sights for a Travelling Law-school are the establishments where the business of the government is done. You already know that most of the business of a State government is managed for the whole State in buildings and offices located in the capital city of the State. Just so, most of the business of the national government is conducted at Washington.

The foremost government building is the Capitol, and it is useful to remember that capital, spelled with an *a*) means a city, but capitol (spelled with an *o*) means a building where the business of a government is done. The Capitol at Washington is a magnificent white marble edifice at the southerly end of the city, crowned with a dome which can be seen glistening in the sunshine from afar. In this Capitol the two houses of Congress meet to make laws for the nation, just as the Legislature of Massachusetts meets in the State House at Boston to make laws for the State. The House of Representatives is composed of members chosen by the people all over the land; the Senate is composed of senators chosen two from each State by its legislature. As there are more than three hundred representatives, and only seventy-six senators, the representatives' hall is much the larger; but both halls are spacious and beautifully furnished. The two Houses commence business early in December every winter, and are busy until spring or summer discussing and passing laws; but they can only make laws about those very general, national things which belong to the Federal Government. They must not meddle with the subjects which belong to the State legislatures meeting in the capital cities of the States.

In the Capitol also is the large hall of the Supreme

Court, fitted with elegant mahogany furniture. As we enter it we shall find a range of seats in curved form near the doors for visitors. These seats are fenced by a railing, beyond which is a space furnished with tables and chairs and occupied by the lawyers. Beyond this space is a raised " bench," at which the nine judges sit, facing the lawyers. The duty of these judges is to decide questions about the United States laws. If people do not understand the laws of Congress, or will not obey them, a lawsuit is brought, lawyers are employed to state the questions to the judges, and the judges explain the law and decide the case. There are similar courts in all the States; and the Washington judges do not meddle with the questions which belong to the State courts to decide.

In the Capitol are also many other interesting things. A grand library so crowded full of books that one can hardly turn around in it; a magnificent rotunda adorned with paintings of Revolutionary history and surmounted with the dome, from which persons who clamber up the lofty stairs obtain a grand view; a collection of statues; a pair of bronze doors bearing historical pictures of exquisite workmanship;

beautiful frescoed halls (where you can buy photographs of almost everything) and stairways, and long, curious passages ; many "committee rooms," whither members of Congress go to discuss the new laws they think of making ; a room so beautifully finished in all sorts of marble that it is called the "marble room ;" also very ingenious machinery and apparatus for heating and lighting, and for pumping fresh air into the rooms.

Toward the other end of the city is the President's house. The formal name for this is the Executive Mansion ; but it is commonly called the White-house. It is not modern and elegant like the Capitol, but old-fashioned ; it is, however, a very important building. It is here that the President gives the orders necessary to make sure that the laws of Congress will be obeyed. If people far away, east or west, north or south, refuse to obey the Federal laws, information is sent to the White-house, and the President and chief officers — the "secretaries," or "cabinet," as they are called — consider the case and give directions what shall be done. But the secretaries do not take any part in making laws ; that duty belongs to

Congress and the President. And the President and cabinet do not concern themselves whether people obey State or city laws, but attend only to the national laws. The lower rooms of the White-house are open to visitors, and are attractive, especially the portraits of former Presidents; and the great East room, where the President's famous receptions are given.

The immense amount of business which arises in enforcing the laws of the national government is divided among "departments;" and the buildings allotted to the several departments are interesting. The State department is the office where all the business of the government with foreign countries is managed, under the charge of the Secretary of State. The Treasury department has a fine building near the White-house, where the Secretary of the Treasury manages the money business of the nation, the collection of duties and taxes and payment of salaries and debts. Here are numerous rooms filled with innumerable clerks busily employed in writing the government's accounts.

And here are to be seen — if we can obtain leave —the printing-presses which make the national bank-notes, the beautiful government bonds, and the treasury notes, and also a banking-room and money-vaults containing immense stores of money of all kinds.

The Post-office department has charge of carrying mails throughout the whole country; for this, being a general subject, is managed at Washington. The States do not meddle with it. The most interesting room is the dead-letter office. Hither are sent all letters whose owners cannot be found; and here is a museum of queer things which have been found in "dead letters."

The Interior department has charge of business all over the country, especially at the West; such as governing the Indians, taking the census of the people, selling lands to immigrants, and giving patents for inventions.

The museum of the Patent office contains models and samples of almost every machine or apparatus; and whoever invents anything new may deposit it here and obtain an exclusive right to make and sell it for seventeen years. The War and Navy departments and department of Justice are less entertaining to visitors, but they are very important.

There is also what is called the department of Agriculture. Its business is to assist the farmers. Suppose in some part of the country all the corn is wilting and dying, and the farmers cannot discover the cause. It would be proper for them to write and send specimens to the department of Agriculture, and some learned man there would study the matter. He would perhaps examine the plants with a powerful microscope, and find that they were infested with a tiny insect. Then he would try experiments till he discovered a cure; and the department would send word to the farmers what to do to save their crops.

There are in Washington many interesting things which have not much connection with government: a Smithsonian Institution which has collected a useful library and museum of natural science; an Army Surgical Museum for showing doctors the ways in which soldiers are wounded in battle and how they may be cured, with the largest library of medical books in the world; two fine conservatories, or nurseries of flowers and plants, one, managed for Congress, not far from the Capitol, the other, managed

for the President, at the White-house ; the Corcoran
Art Gallery of fine paintings : a National Observatory
for studying the stars; busy newspaper offices, where
news of whatever is done by the public officers is sent
to all the great cities. There is no place where in a
few weeks' visit an American can learn so much as in
Washington that is new and useful. And by a short
and pleasant steamboat sail one can reach Mount
Vernon, the home of George Washington, the Revolutionary commander and first President, for whom the
city was named, and there can see the memorials of
his life, and visit his grave.

XII.—CHOOSING OFFICERS.

VERY different ideas have prevailed in different countries upon the best way of forming a government and choosing rulers. The American idea is to have the government planned by wise men whom the people choose for that express purpose, and to have the chief officers chosen by the people.

Another idea has been that rulers are ordained by Almighty God — or, as is sometimes said, that kings rule by "divine right " — and that they should enforce the laws of God found in the Bible. Some rulers have become such by what may be called "the right of the strongest :" an able general has organized a powerful army, conquered the country, and proclaimed himself king or emperor, and the people have submitted rather than contend with the army. As ancient military kings generally made arrangements to have their sons succeed them, there arose an idea that royal power should be inherited as property is. Many persons believe that government ought to be managed by the wisest and best men of the country ; which would be an excellent plan if there were any certain way of knowing who are the wisest and best. The plan of electing rulers gives the people opportunity to choose their wisest and best men if they will take the pains to do so. In this country, although the people do not vote for nearly all officers, they vote for so many, and those who are elected understand so well the necessity of doing as the people wish in appointing others, that, practically, the government is organized and the officers are selected chiefly according to the popular wish. This plan would perhaps not be so good for other nations as the modes they adopt, but it pleases the Americans. The wisest and best men are not always chosen ; but the people obey so much more willingly the officers whom they have elected, and the laws passed by their representatives,

that governing is simpler, easier and cheaper than
it could be under the strongest men or than it might
be under the wisest and best.

Thus in this country the President is chosen almost
directly by the people ; and they can choose one
every four years. The Governors of States are chosen
by the people, and so are representatives in Congress
and members of both houses of State legislatures ;
and their terms are short — mostly two years. Judges,
in many States, and in all, chief officers of various
kinds, are chosen by the people.   The choosing is
done at elections ; the grown men come each with a
little folded paper called his "ballot," in which is
written (so that no one can see unless the voter
chooses to show it) the names of the officers he
prefers ; these ballots are dropped in a box called the
"ballot box," and are afterwards counted ; and the
men whose names appear on the most ballots become
the officers, for they are the ones preferred by the
most voters.

The system, to be sure, does not include senators
of the United States, who are chosen by the State
legislatures ; or judges and chief officers of the United

States, and those of some States who are appointed by the President, or the Governors. And a voter cannot always vote for the man he prefers: he has to choose among those nominated by a " caucus," or " convention; " but in one way or another the people exercise indirectly a powerful influence over the choice of officers whom they do not elect. Indeed, the form of choosing a president is that the people in the various States elect a few of their wisest and best men, called " electors," to meet and choose a president; but really the people make the choice, and the electors merely vote for the man whom they believe the people of their State prefer.

If we should visit foreign countries and examine their governments, we should find that this idea of a choice of rulers by the people is steadily winning favor, especially in the most intelligent and prosperous nations. In England, anciently, some kings claimed to reign by divine right, others by conquest. But in modern times the crown is "inherited." Victoria became queen by right of birth, and, when she dies, her eldest son will be king; not because he is better qualified than any one else to rule, but because (in England) it is thought right that his mother's rank and authority, like her money or lands, should descend to him. But at this day the English people have more real power than the queen. In Parliament, as in Congress, there are two houses; and it is true that the members of the House of Lords, which resembles our Senate, are not chosen, but inherit their rank from their fathers; but the House of Commons, which resembles our House of Representatives, is, chosen by popular election, and it is this house which controls all the money, and holds the chief power. The queen cannot do anything of consequence in the government. She can only choose some member of Parliament to be her Prime Minister; he, like our President, appoints a cabinet; and the Prime Minister and cabinet decide what shall be done. The orders are given in the queen's name, and she signs many of the more important papers, holds a very elevated rank, and is allowed a large income; but the real governing is done chiefly by the men whom the people choose for the House of Commons, or those whom the Commons are willing to sustain in the cabinet.

England has not a written constitution, but its government proceeds according to laws of Parliament and old customs ; hence the growth of the people's right to choose rulers has been gradual, though steady. In France and in Germany the governments were formed anew about twelve years ago, and popular rights were introduced distinctly. France is a republic, organized by a written constitution. The country is divided into departments resembling our States, and they manage local matters, while the Republic governs affairs of general interest. This resembles the American plan. In France, however, the general government establishes a religion and maintains a system of education, an extensive police force and a burdensome army, and controls the newspapers ; while in America such matters are either governed by the States or let alone.

The chief officer of France is a President chosen for seven years, not by the people, but by the National Assembly. This is as if Congress chose our President ; for the National Assembly answers to Congress. It has two houses, a Chamber of Deputies, like the House of Representatives, except that it

is about half as large again, and a Senate which is
almost four times as large as the Senate at Washington.   The deputies are chosen by popular vote in the
departments, one for each *arrondissement*, much as
our representatives are chosen throughout the States,
one in each congressional district. Senators hold
office for life, instead of for six years as in this country. The mode of choosing them is perplexing. Besides the National Assembly, there is a Council of
State, which assists either house in framing laws
wisely and carefully, and gives advice upon any questions or proposed decrees submitted by the President.
There is no similar body in England or in our Federal government. The President has the co-operation
of ministers of State in the performance of his duties,
but their offices are not called " departments," as at
Washington. In France a department is a division
of the country. Each department has its General Council resembling a State Legislature. The
members of a General Council are chosen by the
people, but choose their own presiding officers, as is
done in our legislatures. The *préfet* of a department,
who corresponds to a governor, is appointed ; but

mayors are elected by the various municipal councils.

The German empire has been formed by a number of kingdoms which have retained their power to manage local affairs, uniting by a written Constitution under an Imperial government which manages general subjects, such as citizenship, passports, commerce and duties on imports, coinage, paper money and banking, patents and copyrights, railways, post-offices and telegraphs, etc.

The general laws are made by a Federal Council, much like our Senate, but somewhat smaller (its members are appointed by the kingdoms which they represent, and all the delegates from one kingdom cast their votes as a unit), co-operating with an Imperial Diet, much like our House of Representatives, but somewhat larger (its members are chosen by the people throughout the empire). There is no election of President; whoever is King of Prussia for the time being is President of the German Empire — German Emperor, he is called. This is as if the governor of some chief State were always to be President of the United States. In Switzerland also, as was explained in the first lesson to the Travelling Law-school, the people have a large share in choosing rulers. And it is probable that this principle of popular elections will grow and extend in time to come.

FAMOUS TRIALS

FAMOUS TRIALS.

I. — AUNT SYLVIA'S WILL: FORGERY.

THERE was once a lady named Sylvia Howland,
who was growing old without having been
married, but was very rich. She took her niece,
named Hetty, to live with her as an adopted daughter. This niece had inherited from her mother who
was dead, a little property, but it was not much; her
father had obtained almost all the mother's property,
and by means of it and his success in business had
become even richer than the aunt. In course of time
aunt Sylvia made a will giving her money to her niece.
She gave this will to her niece to keep; and when a
few years later the aunt died, the niece expected that
the property would come to her. But it was then
found that aunt Sylvia had made a later will, giving
the property quite differently.

7

A will is a paper saying how property shall be given after the owner's death. Most persons wish to use what they own as long as they live ; they cannot therefore give it away during lifetime. The law allows writing down one's "will"; that is, one's *wish* as to what shall be done with the property one leaves, and the property must be given to the persons named in the will. If one makes several wills, the one made last is the one to be obeyed. Thus when aunt Sylvia's second will was found, every one said: "Oh, the old lady changed her mind towards the last, and thought she would not give her whole fortune to her niece." And ordinarily any one has a right to change his mind and make a later will, and this overthrows all that were earlier made.

But suppose a person has made a solemn contract not to change the will first made? Suppose aunt Sylvia, for example, made a bargain with niece Hetty that the niece should have her money when she died; ought she to change her mind secretly, and make a new will without telling Hetty of it? Certainly not.

Niece Hetty declared that she and aunt Sylvia had made such a bargain. Her story was somewhat like this : " Aunt Sylvia was displeased with my father for his taking so much of my mother's fortune away from me. She said that my mother was a Howland, and her money came from the Howlands, and ought to have gone to me, her daughter. She told me she was determined my father should not get any more Howland money if she could prevent it; and that if I would make a will giving whatever I should leave when I died to people satisfactory to her, she would make her will leaving her money to me. Her motive was to make sure that my father would not inherit her money or mine. I did make just such a will as she wished. She dictated her will to me, and I wrote it on a slate, and copied it on sheets of paper. Then she signed it. She gave me her will to keep, and I gave her mine. And we each promised the other not to change our wills."

The people who would have aunt Sylvia's money under the second will, said : " All that is only your story; you have nothing to show to prove it."

" Yes, I have," said niece Hetty; " aunt Sylvia dictated another paper, which I copied for her and she signed, telling the whole matter."

And sure enough there were found two copies of a paper called the "second page" of the will, in niece Hetty's handwriting, but signed with aunt Sylvia's name, declaring very solemnly that the first will should never be changed. But those who wished the second will to be established would not believe that aunt Sylvia ever signed this "second page." They accused niece Hetty of having "forged" aunt Sylvia's name; that is, of having written the name herself, imitating the aunt's handwriting.

Forgery is imitating a person's signature, or making a fictitious document in order to obtain property. This is a grave crime, and severely punished whenever detected. And it can nearly always be detected. Almost all business is managed, property sold or money paid, by means of little written papers to which people sign their names. Young and inexperienced persons when they see business men dashing off their signatures to checks, notes, receipts and orders, are apt to imagine it very easy and safe to imitate a man's signature, and by that means get some of his property. A small boy who entered a lawyer's office as messenger, but had never been taught anything about forgery, saw the lawyer sign checks and send them to the bank, where the money was always paid ; and he supposed he could get money for himself in that way. So one day he signed the lawyer's name to a check for ten dollars and presented it at the bank. As the cashier was good natured and saw that the boy was ignorant, he only laughed at him, tore up the check, and told the lawyer that he had better teach his errand boy something about forgery. If he had been a stern man, or had thought that the boy understood what he was doing, he would have sent him to prison. Business men, especially clerks in banks, acquire great skill in knowing signatures and detecting imitations or forgeries. For no two natural handwritings are precisely alike. Almost every person has a peculiar way of making some letters. Besides this there is what is called a general character of each hand which distinguishes it from others. Even when one person imitates another's signature and does so very skilfully, there will be some minute differences. Ordinary people may be deceived, but those who are trained in the scientific ways of detecting forgeries can almost always distinguish a genuine signature from an imitated one.

Accordingly there was a long trial to ascertain whether aunt Sylvia really signed the "second page" of her will, or niece Hetty forged her name. For certain reasons the trial stopped before this was learned. But it is very certain that if there was an attempt at forgery it did not succeed. The trial shows that forgery is exceedingly difficult and dangerous.

Not only is there a difference between two persons' handwritings, but any one person scarcely ever signs his name twice precisely alike. You can try the experiment by writing your name on each of two not very thick pieces of paper, and then laying one over the other against a window pane. See whether one signature will exactly fit the other. The persons who accused niece Hetty of forging aunt Sylvia's name said that she had done it by " tracing it ;" that is, by putting the genuine signature of the will against the window and laying the other paper over, so that she could see the name through it, and then tracing letters on the second paper to correspond precisely with those underneath. If she did so her plan was ingenious, but it made the false signature too much like the real one. A learned professor testified that he had calculated the matter mathematically, and that there was only one chance among two thousand six hundred and sixty-six millions of millions of millions that aunt Sylvia could have written her name three times as precisely alike as it appeared upon the will and the two copies of the " second page."

The microscope is of great use in detecting forgeries. If the forger sketches the name first with a pencil, and writes with ink over the pencil, as is often done to make the imitation more perfect, the microscope will reveal the lead-pencil marks; or, if the forger has rubbed these out, the microscope will reveal traces of the rubbing.

A sea-captain once hired a chronometer for use on his voyage and signed a printed receipt for it; but his ship was wrecked and he never brought the chronometer back. The chronometer man brought a law suit, for he claimed that the sea-captain had promised to pay for it if it should be lost. He produced his receipt, and, behold, it contained two lines written in a blank space above the captain's signature, making just such a promise. The sea-captain swore that these lines were not written when he signed the receipt, and declared that they must have been forged afterward. But the lawyer for the chronometer man said: "Look at the writing under a microscope." This was done, and showed that the top of a letter in the sea-captain's name ran up into the bottom of a letter in the written promise, and that the inks of the two letters had mingled while they were fresh, form-'ing a sort of puddle. In other words, the sea-captain had signed his name while the ink of the promise to pay for the chronometer was still wet.

Another way of using the microscope is to magnify two writings upon large screens, and take photographs of the images appearing on the screens. When these photographs are compared, all the minute peculiarities of each handwriting can be very plainly seen.

Some skilful persons say that every one's hand trembles a very little while he is writing, and that no two hands tremble precisely alike. This trembling —nerve-tremor, it is called—can be seen by the microscope in the letters; thus if one should see that the aunt's name signed underneath a paper in the niece's handwriting showed the same nerve-tremor with what was written by the niece, he would declare that the niece wrote the name.

Forgeries are detected by various accidental circumstances. A cadet at West Point was once accused of forging a letter which was written on a half sheet of note paper; and when his desk was searched the other half of the same sheet was found among his stationery. His accusers considered this strong proof. Suppose a will dated 1870 were written on paper having a peculiar watermark, and the manufacturer of the paper were to say that he did not begin making the paper with that mark until 1878; it would be natural to think that the will was forged. Some persons who were plotting to forge a deed thought it would be shrewd to put a sixpence under the wax seal, and did so ; and when they testified about the signing and sealing, they said that the deed they saw signed had a sixpence put under the seal. They thought the lawyers would break the wax, and when they found a sixpence there would believe all the rest of the story. The wax was broken, and the sixpence found. But the lawyer who was against the deed said, "Examine the date of the sixpence!" And, behold the sixpence was dated several years later than the deed. This proved the forgery.

Forgers are often detected by little mistakes they make, especially mistakes in spelling. If a teacher knew that a boy in his school was wont to misspell *money* thus, "munney," and if this boy should one day bring what seemed to be a letter from his father to the teacher, asking the teacher to give the boy some "munney" for Christmas, would not the teacher suspect that the pupil had written the letter himself and signed his father's name? Well, this actually happens in law suits.

A person named Alexander learned that a man of the same name had died leaving property but no heirs. He thought he would present himself as heir and claim the estate. He forged a parcel of family letters describing himself as heir. But the lawyer against him observed that several words were misspelled alike in all the letters. When the case was tried the lawyer asked that Alexander write something from the judge's dictation, and he gave to be dictated a paragraph containing these same words. The unlucky forger misspelled them all in the same way. Then they showed him what he had done, and accused him plumply of having forged the letters; and he at length confessed. Thus it is almost impossible to make fictitious papers or signatures without incurring disgrace and punishment.

II.—COLVIN AND THE BOORNS: CON-
FESSIONS.

MOST persons when they hear that a culprit has confessed his crime, consider that of course he must be guilty. "What is the need of any' proof if the man has confessed?" Many novels and stories are written upon the idea that an admission of guilt is abundantly sufficient to warrant punishing the person who makes it. But lawyers and judges have observed that confessions are very often fictitious.

This is well illustrated by the strange story of Colvin and the Boorns.

Seventy years ago there lived in Manchester, Vt., a family named Boorn, composed of father and mother, two sons Jesse and Stephen, and a daughter who was married to a man named Colvin. This Colvin was of weak and gradually decaying mind; did but little to support himself and wife; was wont to

ramble away, no one knew whither, for days and
weeks at a time; and Jesse and Stephen Boorn
found fault with him and treated him unkindly for
his idle ways and because he and his wife depended
on the Boorn family for much of their support.

At length Colvin disappeared on one of his erratic
excursions, and failed to return.   Some months
afterwards the mystery was explained by finding that
he had strayed, in a demented way, to New Jersey;
but at the time when our story opens he was missing,
and the neighbors were beginning to inquire what
had become of him, and to discuss whether the
Boorn boys could have carried their ill treatment of
him so far as to kill him.   No wonder that when
people were talking of such an affair some of them
should dream of it; and one old man dreamed
"three nights running," that Colvin came to his bed-
side and disclosed that he had been murdered, and
that his body was buried in an old, disused potato-
cellar.   The story of this dream led people to ran-
sack that cellar, and some bones were found.   These,
as was ultimately shown, were remains of some
animal; but when they were first found they were

supposed to be Colvin's, and a great excitement arose against Jesse and Stephen Boorn; nearly every one believing that they had killed their brother-in-law to prevent his continuing a burden on the family, and that his spirit had revealed the crime by the dream! They were at once arrested and placed in jail, where many of the neighbors visited them, urging them to confess.

And they did confess. Jesse first described how the three were at work together in the field, when Stephen beat Colvin senseless with a club, after which the body was carried to the deserted cellar and buried. Stephen, who at first denied the charge, afterward made a written confession, substantially supporting Jesse's story; he, however, laid blame on Colvin, saying that the latter began the quarrel and struck the first blow.

Upon these two confessions — there was scarcely any other evidence — the two Boorns were convicted of murder. But it is very common to show some mercy to offenders who confess crimes and aid in bringing others to justice, and the legislature, probably for this reason, changed Jesse's punishment to imprisonment for life; leaving Stephen sentenced to death.

Now comes the strange part of the story. Both the confessions were false! Colvin was alive and well all the while! As a last hope, Stephen Boorn's counsel published an advertisement asking whether any person could give information of the missing man. This came to the notice of people in New Jersey, who sent word that a person resembling Colvin was working as hired man on a farm in Dover, in that State. This man was brought to Vermont, and sure enough, he was the veritable Colvin. Then the excitement was greater than ever. Crowds of people rushed into the court-room to see the returned wanderer. Cannon were fired in honor of the news, and there was great rejoicing. The two prisoners were of course very soon set free.

What can have been the motive of the two Boorns for making these false confessions?

Every one around them was urging them to confess, and the probability is that they believed they would surely be found guilty—perhaps, indeed, they were not certain but that Colvin had died somewhere of a

beating received from them — and that they hoped
by confessing to obtain lighter punishment. This
hope indeed was realized in Jesse's case; in Stephen's
it was disappointed.

Nowadays courts and judges are very strict in for-
bidding people to urge a prisoner to confess his crime.

The rule is that if he makes confession entirely of
his own accord it may be received against him; but
if he was urged, if any promises or threats were made
to induce him to speak, what he says goes for nothing. The famous case of the Boorns has saved a
great many accused persons from being convicted
upon confessions wrested from them by policemen
and jailers. In ancient times and foreign lands it
has been common to even torture prisoners in order
to induce them to confess. Nothing of this kind is
allowed by our law. Prisoners must be treated
humanely, and left wholly at liberty to confess or
deny as they choose.

False confessions are made from various motives.
Persons who were poor, friendless and unhappy,
have been known to accuse themselves of a crime in
order to be imprisoned, or even in order to be put to

death.   After the famous " Great Fire of London," a
Frenchman came forward with a story that he kin-
dled the fire to earn a bribe which had been paid
him for doing so; and he was executed for the supposed crime.   Probably he had become weary of life,
yet could not quite resolve to destroy himself.   Some
persons have such a diseased ambition to be talked
about that they will make false confessions.   About
twenty years ago there was a mysterious murder in
New York city, of a dentist named Burdell; and
while police and people were making every effort to
detect the offenders, a person avowed himself guilty.
But inquiry showed he had no part in the crime; he
only said so to obtain the temporary notoriety.   The like
has been done in many instances.   A fit of insanity,
or of drunkenness, may lead a person to confess
something which he has not done.

Sometimes, no doubt, persons make fictitious confessions in order to disgrace or injure others whom
they charge with having taken part in the offence,
and sometimes the opposite happens — a relative or
friend will assume a crime in order to shield the real
offender.   For example: In England, once, two

brothers were suspected of a highway robbery. They were in fact guilty, but a third brother, younger than they, confessed that he committed it, upon which he was seized and they were let alone. They escaped to America, after which the younger brother retracted his confession and made clear proof that he was innocent. Of course he could not be punished for the robbery which he did not commit; and his guilty brothers could not be, for they were out of reach.

Suppose a man enters the police office in a Massachusetts town and says : " Several years ago I stole money in Boston, and my conscience troubles me so much about it that I have come to give myself up to be punished." If the officers are not shrewd — if they take it for granted that because the man has confessed he must be guilty — they will very likely send the man to Boston to be tried; and of course they must feed him and pay his car fare on the journey. When the party reach Boston the officers find that no one knows anything about any such theft as their prisoner confessed, and they have to set him at liberty. Thus he has been carried to Boston without having to pay anything; which is just what he wished.

Whenever we hear or read that a person has admitted himself guilty of a crime, we are not to be absolutely sure, at once, that he is so, but must remember that fictitious confessions are not uncommon.

III.—THE STORY OF JENNIE DIVER:
STEALING.

JENNIE DIVER was a poor girl born in Ireland about one hundred and fifty years ago. Her original name was Mary Young. After her parents died, she went to London and tried to earn a living; but all this occurred while yet there were very few day schools or books, and no Sunday-schools or children's magazines or newspapers; hence the poor girl had not been taught anything but sewing; and she could not get enough employment. She was nearly starving when she made the acquaintance of some thieves who invited her to join their society, promising to teach her how to steal. There is a famous story of a poor boy in London named Oliver Twist, who fell among thieves in nearly the same way; but he had knowledge or good conscience enough to run away from them the moment he found that their business was stealing; and after various hard adventures, he was adopted by a good family and reared to be useful and happy. The story of his struggles and success is very interesting. This girl consented to remain with the thieves. They gave her the name Jennie Diver. She practised the tricks they taught her, and at length became very skilful. For example, she one day went to a church where she heard there would be a crowd, and watching the people until she saw a gentleman wearing a diamond ring, she held out her hand to him. The gentleman seeing a young lady extending her hand as if she wished to be helped up the steps, reached his hand to assist her, and while he was doing so she contrived to twist off the ring. At another time she fitted herself with false arms and hands and attended church, and while she sat with her false hands folded, apparently listening to the service, her real hands were busy stealing the watches of the ladies sitting near her.

These are only examples of a great many tricks she practised. For a long time she was successful and escaped detection, but at length a lady feeling Jennie's hand in her pocket taking out some money, caught her by the gown, and she was arrested and taken to court to be tried. She was found guilty. At that time the punishment for stealing (more than a shilling's worth) was death, and poor Jennie was accordingly hung. At the present day she would only be sent to prison and fined, but even these punishments disgrace any one for the rest of life.

Young persons are more likely to be tempted to ' steal than to commit any other crime; and often stealing seems easy and safe. It really is very dangerous and disgraceful. The story of Jennie Diver shows that if so cunning and dexterous a girl as she could not escape detection, an ordinary boy or girl cannot hope to. The money you covet may seem within safe reach; the fruit desired may be temptingly handy; the jewelry you admire, the watch, the dress, the book you would take, may appear to be unguarded; and often a person is not detected the first time. Generally, however, a thief is at last caught, and is disgraced for life.

One reason for this is, that detectives are even more ingenious than ordinary thieves. A store-

keeper who suspects a clerk of stealing will sometimes mark a piece of money or a bill with minute,
peculiar marks, and put it in the drawer. If, next
day, he searches the clerk's pockets and finds there
the marked money, he knows that the clerk has been
stealing from the drawer. Many thieves have been
caught by a detective who pretended to assist them,
but really was watching to see what they would do.
For instance, a man was once suspected of stealing
his neighbor's cattle by means of branding them
with his mark in place of the mark of the real owner.
—Ask some grown person to explain to you how cattle
on the Western prairies are branded with their owners'
tokens.—One day a detective in disguise came to
the farmer's house and asked if he did not wish
to hire a herdsman.

The farmer said "yes," and questioned the dis-
guised detective, who answered all the questions so
satisfactorily that the farmer hired him. He then
began watching everything which the farmer did,
until at length he detected him in changing marks of
cattle. Then he threw off his disguise, arrested the
farmer, and took him to court to be tried. However

safe everything may appear, no one can ever know but that there is an ingenious trap set for him by detectives. Another reason why stealing is so dangerous is that persons cannot sell or even show stolen property anywhere in the neighborhood without risk of being asked where they got it. It is considered evidence of stealing that a person is found with the stolen property and cannot give an explanation showing that he came by it innocently. Another reason is, that even if a thief is not actually detected, he is usually suspected, and when the neighbors once begin to suspect a person of stealing they will not employ him, invite him to their houses, or make friends with him any way.

Young persons are sometimes perplexed to know what they ought to do in case of finding anything which has been lost. A great many stories are related about this. The rule is, that whoever finds a lost thing ought to return it to the owner; but if the owner cannot be found, the finder has a better right to the thing than any one else. If one should find a purse of money lying on the sidewalk, and should pick it up saying to himself, " I will hide this money and spend it," this would be stealing. But if he should take it meaning to advertise it and make inquiries of the owner, there would be no theft: and after he had made proper efforts to find the owner without success, he could lawfully spend the money himself. The chief question is, What was the intention in the finder's mind? This is sometimes difficult to be ascertained.

In one instance a horse jumped over his owner's fence and ran along the highway several miles, when he was caught by a farmer. This farmer put the animal in his barn and began to use him, driving him to market and to meeting, etc., but he did so publicly. At length the owner heard where the horse was, and made a complaint for stealing. But the judges said that the farmer had used the horse so openly that he probably did not intend to steal it, but was only using it till the owner should appear. True, he ought to have made inquiries, but omitting to make inquiries is not as bad as theft. In an instance in a city there was a little girl who owned a canary bird which she kept in a cage hanging against the fence in the yard. Some children who lived next door unhooked the cage, carried it into their house and hid it; but they did this in joke, and to tease their neighbor, and when they thought they had kept it long enough to frighten her, they put it back. However, they were accused of stealing; but the judge said that taking a thing temporarily for fun or mischief is not stealing, though it may be very wrong. In Iowa a flood once swept away a great part of a village, and all sorts of articlés were left on the banks of the stream when the water subsided. A man found some clothes and some valuable papers. The clothes were not marked, the papers bore the owner's name, but both belonged to the same person. The finder carried them all home. Not long afterwards he was prosecuted for stealing the clothing. But it appeared that he had made inquiries for the owner of the papers, therefore the judges said that he would probably have given up the clothing as soon as he learned the owner, and therefore he must be acquitted. Intention to appropriate the thing to one's own use is necessay in theft.

Accordingly, if a person who finds anything behaves as if he meant to hide it and use it himself, he is likely to be pronounced a thief. For instance, when some workmen were digging in a street one of them found a roll of about two hundred dollars in bank notes, sticking between the stones. His duty was to make known that he had found the money, and to inquire for the owner. Instead of this he concealed it and spent part of it the same day. The judges said that this was stealing. There was once a man who dropped a sack of coffee out of his wagon while he was driving along a country road. About a mile beyond he missed it, and then returned, looking for it, and asking persons whom he met. One of these very persons had found the sack and hidden it, apparently meaning to come for it some time when he could safely do so, and when the wagoner inquired of him he denied having seen it. However, he was caught, and the judges said he must be punished as a thief. All honest persons who find anything of value, endeavor to restore it to the owner.

IV.—LOUIS VICTOR'S SUFFERINGS:
PHOTOGRAPHS.

THERE was once an orphan asylum called the "Shepherd's Fold." Children who had not parents to care for them were sent there to be reared, and benevolent people gave money from time to time, to buy food and clothing for the children and pay for their education. At length it became suspected that the manager was keeping this money for himself and was neglecting his little wards. The officers of a society for Prevention of Cruelty heard of this, and they visited the asylum, and found that it was true; the poor little children were nearly starved, and were shockingly ragged, dirty and sickly. The officers immediately sent for carriages, put the children in them and drove with them to another asylum, where they could be fed, washed and clothed. And in a short time the selfish, cruel manager was tried for his

34

misconduct, and was found guilty, and sent to prison.
The officers were greatly helped in proving that he
was guilty, by photographs of one of the children,
named Louis Victor.   Before this boy was sent to
the asylum his friends had his photograph taken; it
showed him to be a strong, hearty, fine-looking boy
about three years old, sitting up very erect, holding
a little gun, and wearing a bright, animated expression
of face.   When the officers brought him away from
the Shepherd's Fold they had his photograph taken
again; it showed him very emaciated and sick, lying
on a little couch so weak that he could not lift his
head, and looking as if he were at the point of dying
of· starvation.   On the trial the witnesses testified
that Louis had scarcely any food at the Fold, and
that he grew sickly for want of nourishment; but
recovered soon after he was taken to the better asylum.   Then these two photographs were shown to
the jury.   The judges said that photographs were a
very good means of exhibiting little Louis Victor's
sufferings.   Thus we see that photographs may be
very useful in trials in court.   And in fact they are
often used both in explaining how the person or thing

photographed looked on some former day; and also
in detecting and arresting persons who have run away.

Another trial in which a boy's photograph was useful in obtaining justice for him, has occurred. A
farmer took the lad to live in his family, and work in
his house and upon the farm. The boy did not rise
in the mornings so early as his employer wished, and
the latter one morning went up to the boy's sleeping-
room, and while he was in bed and undressed, whipped
him very severely and cruelly. The friends of the
boy immediately had a photograph taken, showing
how his back was bruised and wounded by the blows,
and then brought a lawsuit against the harsh employer.
When the jury saw the picture, they said that the
man should pay five hundred dollars damages. If
there had not been a picture taken at the time, most
likely the farmer and his wife and children would
have sworn that the boy was hurt only very little, and
the jury would not have known whether to believe
them or the friends of the boy.

There lived in Baltimore ten or twelve years ago,
a man of the simple name of Goss, and one bearing
the more complex name Udderzook. They were

brothers-in-law. The man of simple name seems to have been of confiding mind, the other to have possessed a cunning, crafty disposition. They united in a plan of making money by cheating insurance companies; thus: What are called "life insurance policies," for $25,000, were taken out on the life of Goss — that is, the insurance companies agreed to pay his family the money when he should die — then the two obtained the body of a man looking somewhat like Goss, laid it in Goss' paint-shop, and set fire to the shop; then Goss ran away, while Udderzook staid by the fire, assisted in bringing out the dead and burned body, made believe to lament and cry because his dear brother-in-law Goss had been burned to death, and in course of time demanded the insurance money from the companies.

Meanwhile Goss wandered about awhile, and at length strayed into Pennsylvania, calling himself "Wilson," and waiting for Udderzook to collect the money and bring him his share. But Udderzook had a different plan. He came to where Goss, called "Wilson," was hiding, coaxed him to take a walk in a wild forest, and there killed him. This was very crafty and cunning, for he thought that no one who knew Goss would ever look for him in those woods, because they all supposed he had been burned in the paint-shop; and that if the body should ever be found by the people of the neighborhood, they would suppose it to be the stranger they had heard called "Wilson," and no one would particularly care. But there was a photograph of the murdered man. When he went to the insurance company's office about his policy, he and the agent became friendly, and one day they had their likenesses taken on one card, side by side. This photograph was shown, as it happened, to people who had seen the man called "Wilson," and they recognized the companion of the agent in the picture as their Mr. "Wilson," though really Goss. Thus the crime was detected, and the murderer was found guilty (and hung) by means of a photograph. No matter how cunning a person's plans of committing a crime are, there is very apt to be some little accident which leads to his exposure and punishment.

Some of the ways in which pictures are used in searching for criminals who have run away, are curious. Suppose that a clerk in a bank steals a large sum of money and travels to the South or West. The police officers immediately inquire for a picture of the man. When they obtain one, they have it photographed, printing a great many copies. Under each is printed a description of the clerk, and an offer of a reward to any person who will report having seen him. Circulars containing the picture and reward are sent to ever so many people living in the part of the country to which the clerk has gone. In a great many cases some person meets him, notices that he resembles the picture, and sends word to the police, and they come and arrest him. Of course such runaways try various means of disguising themselves so as not to be recognized, but that is a very difficult thing to do. Thus a criminal can very often be detected at a great distance from home by means of distributing copies of his photograph.

A man in England robbed another of his watch and sold the chain, and then took passage to this country by a sail vessel. The police obtained his photograph and showed it to the jeweler, and he said, "That is the likeness of the man who sold me the chain." They then took the jeweler and the picture with them, and sailed in a swifter vessel to this country, arriving before the criminal could. When his vessel reached the wharf the English policemen were standing there, waiting to arrest him, and having the photograph to prove that he was the guilty man. A fugitive criminal named Chastine Cox, was caught by a newspaper reporter, in Boston, by means of his photograph.

Of course photographs must not be used in trials unless they are faithful and accurate. Sometimes they are unskilfully or carelessly taken, and do not represent the original correctly. Sometimes they are purposely distorted; a picture can be taken as a caricature, which will be very absurd.

A remarkable instance of this is the case of a skilful photographer who contrived means of casting upon a card a dim, shadowy appearance resembling a ghost as people commonly imagine ghosts. He advertised that he would take pictures of the spirits of persons who were dead! And there were people who believed that this was possible, and who paid him a good deal of money for such pictures.

A gentleman whose wife was dead, came for one, and was taken with a faint outline of a lady standing behind him, which the photographer pretended was a likeness of the wife.

A lady who had lost her daughter was taken with an indistinct, filmy representation of a little girl standing by her side; and he told her that it was the daughter.

Nothing of this kind could be true, therefore before long the artist was prosecuted for swindling. If pictures representing ghosts can be made, of course there may be ways in which a deceitful person could make very untruthful *cartes de visite*. The judges are careful to allow only veritable likenesses to be used in trials.

Photographs are used in many other ways. In large cities the police officers keep what is called a " Rogues' Gallery," a room in which are hung portraits of thieves, swindlers, and other offenders who have been arrested. These are of great service in identifying criminals. The criminals know this, and some of them make great effort to prevent a good likeness; they twist their faces and limbs so as to look as strange as possible while they are before the camera, and their pictures are very queer. Copies of important papers are often taken by photography. If a building or a bridge falls, and persons hurt by it mean to bring a lawsuit, they often find it convenient to take a photograph showing exactly how it appeared at the time.

V. — AN UNFORTUNATE FRENCHMAN: CIRCUMSTANTIAL EVIDENCE.

WE often read of a person's being condemned upon "circumstantial evidence." What is circumstantial evidence? All readers know what is meant by "direct testimony." When Guiteau was tried there were Mr. Blaine and several other persons who testified that they were at the depot at the time, and saw Guiteau fire the pistol shot at President Garfield. This is an instance of direct testimony, which consists of statements of witnesses who saw the crime committed.

Often, however, persons committing crimes take care not to be seen. In such cases the detectives and policemen collect all the facts or circumstances that can be learned about the offence or the person suspected, and if these circumstances are such as to show that no one but he can have done the deed,

43

and that he must certainly be guilty, he may be punished, although no one saw the act done. Evidence which consists of collecting various suspicious facts and connecting them together to prove a person guilty, is called "circumstantial."

A very interesting story entitled "The Goldsmith of Padua" is probably founded upon a trial of a Frenchman who, about a century ago, came near being hung for counterfeiting upon circumstantial evidence. Various persons to whom he sold goods complained that he came to them and charged them with having paid him in counterfeit money, and made them take back bad gold pieces which he said he had received from them, and give him good ones in exchange. At length this happened with one of his customers named Harris, who had paid Du Moulin seventy-eight pounds in gold pieces. When the payment was made, Du Moulin said that he thought some of the gold pieces were bad, but Harris assured him that all were good, and he accepted them. A few days later, he brought six counterfeit pieces to Harris, and said:

"Here are six of the coins you paid me. They

are counterfeit. I wish you to take them back and give me good money."

Harris examined the coins, and said :

" I am positive that neither of these was in the money I paid to you."

But Du Moulin answered :

" These are some of the very coins I received from you. I put your money in a drawer by itself, and it was kept locked up there until I came to pay it away, when these pieces were found to be bad. I am positive they are the same."

There were some lawsuits between them, the result of which was that Du Moulin swore positively to having kept the coins locked by themselves all the time, and that Harris was compelled to replace them.

The real explanation was that Du Moulin had in his employment a clerk who was one of a party of counterfeiters. This clerk had procured a false key to his master's money drawers, and was accustomed to visit them at night, put in a few counterfeit pieces, and take out an equal number of good ones. But neither Harris, nor Du Moulin, nor any one else had the least suspicion of this.

Harris, who was very angry, believed that Du Moulin was secretly a counterfeiter, and that he had contrived the plan of charging his customers with paying in false money, as an ingenious way of getting the coin which he made exchanged for good. He made a complaint. Du Moulin's drawers were searched, and behold! a good deal more bad money was found, together with some counterfeit tools. Then every one believed that Du Moulin was guilty. He was tried, and upon this circumstantial evidence, was found guilty. He could not explain how the money and the tools came to be in his drawers. But very fortunately the wicked clerk was detected just in season to save the master's life; and he confessed his contrivance for exchanging his counterfeits, and that when he heard that the officers were coming to search the drawers, he put in some of his tools to make the circumstantial evidence against his master stronger.

This illustrates one great danger in trusting to circumstantial evidence. It is that possibly some malicious person may have contrived the suspicious circumstances in order to throw guilt upon the accused man.

In the days of highway robbers, the landlord of an inn was wont to ride forth at evening, and rob travellers; and one night a man whom he had just robbed came to his inn and told the people who were there, how he had been stopped on his way, and despoiled of a purse of twenty guineas.

" But," said he, " my guineas were all marked."

When the landlord, who was in the room, heard this, he trembled and turned pale, for he had paid away one of the guineas, and he thought : When the person to whom I gave that marked guinea hears of the robbery, he will disclose that I gave him the guinea. What shall I say then ? He forthwith plotted a case of circumstantial evidence against one of the waiters of his inn. He crept into the waiter's chamber and hid the purse and the nineteen guineas in the pocket of the waiter's clothes. He then told the gentleman who had been robbed this fictitious story :

" My waiter has lately behaved suspiciously, particularly in showing gold pieces which we do not know how he can have earned. This very evening I gave him a guinea to get it changed. He was gone a long time, and returned saying that no one would give him change. But the guinea which he gave back to me was not the one I had handed him; it was marked as you say yours were. I did not think much about this at the time, and managed to do without the change, but paid away the guinea."

After he had said this, the waiter's room was searched, and the purse and the nineteen guineas were found; and in due time the man who had the twentieth brought it back, and corroborated the story that it had been paid to him by the landlord. Every one believed the poor waiter guilty, and he was hung for the robbery; but about a year afterward the landlord confessed.

There are accounts of a number of cases like this, in which a thief or an enemy has hidden stolen things in an innocent person's trunk or clothing, and then charged him with having stolen them. And even when there is no such malicious plot, it often happens that circumstances make a person appear guilty when he is innocent.

There was a trial of a Mr. Mellon for poisoning his wife, but at the last moment it was discovered that she took the poison of her own accord, because she thought it would make her handsomer. This trial has been written as a novel called *The Law and the Lady*.

There was once an innocent man tried who was only saved by the fact that the real criminal was upon the jury, and he would not consent to a verdict of guilty. This trial is the basis of a novel called *Live it down*.

Eugene Aram and *Sir Theodosius Boughton* are noted novels founded upon cases of false circumstantial evidence.

To allow circumstantial evidence is absolutely necessary, for if it were prohibited entirely, nearly half the crimes would go unpunished. But experienced officers and lawyers are very careful how they trust it, unless it is very clear and strong. Still more ought we to be careful of believing persons to be guilty when we have only heard a story of suspicious circumstances; for there may be some explanation which no one has suggested, but which will show the suspected person innocent.

VI. — MARTIN GUERRE AND ARNAULD DU TILH: PERSONAL IDENTITY.

MANY of my readers will remember the recent and very famous Tichborne Trial. About thirty years ago Roger Charles Tichborne, heir to the great Tichborne estates in England, went travelling abroad, and in 1854, set sail from Rio Janeiro for New York, but the vessel was lost at sea, and every one but his mother accepted the belief that he was drowned. Eleven years afterward a man whose real name was Arthur Orton, arrived in England, pretending to be Roger Charles Tichborne, and claimed the estates. He resembled Tichborne somewhat, and had in some way learned so many facts about Tichborne's life and travels that he could tell a very plausible story; and he deceived many people, including even Tichborne's mother. Two very lengthy and expensive trials were needful before it could be established that he was only a swindler. And even to this day some persons doubt whether he is not the true Tichborne, and was not condemned unjustly.

That a mother should be deceived into accepting a swindler as her son seems very strange, but there is a case stranger yet, in which an impostor deceived a wife into recognizing him as her husband. The true husband's name was Martin Guerre, and he was married to the lady, whose name was Bertrande, when they were only eleven and ten years of age. The affair occurred in France more than three hundred years ago; when such early marriages were allowed. The couple lived very happily for about a dozen years, when Martin Guerre suddenly disappeared. He was last seen walking along the road carrying a bag and stick, and apparently starting on a journey. People supposed that he had become tired of living at home, and had determined to travel and see the world. Nothing was heard of him for eight years. At the end of that time this Martin Guerre (as all the towns-people supposed) was seen coming back through the streets, recognizing his old neighbors and friends, and looking just as he used, except that he had grown stouter and somewhat sunburned, and now wore a heavy beard. He walked directly to his old home, where his wife recognized him as readily as the neighbors had done, and welcomed him very kindly; though he had deserted her so cruelly, she uttered no reproaches, but treated him affectionately.

Of course every one asked Martin Guerre all sorts of questions as to why he went away and where he had been. He said that he became ashamed of knowing so little of the world, and had therefore enlisted in the army; and he gave accounts of sieges and battles in which he had been engaged. He also, in conversation with his friends, reminded them of many occurrences in old times which they had forgotten. To Bertrande in particular, he rehearsed incidents of past years, and seemed perfectly familiar with everything that had happened. For instance, when they awoke on the morning after his arrival, he asked her to "bring me my white breeches trimmed with white silk; you will find them at the bottom of the large beech chest under the linen." She had long forgotten the breeches and even the box, but she found them just as he had described. How was it possible to doubt that a man who came so naturally, who resembled Martin Guerre so closely, and who was so familiar with all the little details of Guerre's life, was in truth Martin Guerre. Yet he was not; he was an impostor; and his real name was Arnauld Du Tilh.

Three years passed away before any one suspected the deception. It then happened that a soldier who had known the real Martin Guerre in the wars, passed through the village, and, upon seeing the false Martin Guerre, declared that he was a cheat. Then arose the famous trial to ascertain the truth. French trials differ from English and American in this respect, that it is common for the judge to question the accused very closely, endeavoring to convict him by his own admissions. The false Martin Guerre was interrogated day after day in the most searching manner; but he answered all questions, and no one could detect error in any of the answers. For example, he gave correctly all details as to his marriage, naming the persons who were present, and the priest who officiated, describing the arrangements and the dresses, and giving the smallest circumstances without hesitation or mistake. After having questioned him, the courts went onward to examine witnesses. The general result of two long investigations was that more than forty witnesses declared positively that the accused was really Martin Guerre; among these were four sisters and two brothers-in-law of Guerre, and many other persons who had known him intimately before his disappearance. These witnesses described a number of personal peculiarities and marks upon the real Guerre, all which were found upon the accused. Upon the other hand about forty-five witnesses were very certain that the accused was not Martin Guerre, but was Arnauld Du Tilh, whom many of them knew very well. All the while the accused continued to meet the witnesses against him with perfect composure and confidence, and to answer all questions frankly and correctly. And upon the whole, the judges were scarcely able to decide; they thought that the testimony was so nearly balanced, and that the man appeared so well, that they could not find him guilty. It is a very important rule of law that every person accused of crime must have "the benefit of the doubt," if there be a reasonable doubt, of his guilt. If an accused person is innocent, or if the jury or the judge doubt whether he is innocent or guilty, he must be set at liberty ; he can be convicted and punished only when there is clear proof that he committed the crime charged against him. In this case the proof was not clear, but was very conflicting and doubtful ; and the judges were about to give the prisoner the benefit of this doubt and therefore acquit him.

But just before such decision was rendered, the real Martin Guerre returned to the town. He recognized his old home, his neighbors, relatives and friends, as his predecessor had done ; inquired for his wife, and on being told that she was attending the trial, which was proceeding in another town, he went thither and presented himself in court. Strange to say, the accused man was not disturbed, but maintained his claim and story as calmly and positively as ever, declaring that the new-comer was an impostor who had been hired to appear by those who were prosecuting the trial against him. And, stranger yet, he seemed to be able to answer questions about the past life of the Guerre family more minutely and accurately

than the second claimant was able to do. But when
the witnesses who had believed him to be Martin
Guerre, were asked to look at the new-comer, they
pronounced in his favor, retracting their former testimony. Thus the four sisters recognized him positively, and the oldest of them, after a moment's
glance, burst into tears and embraced him, crying,
"This, this, is my brother, Martin Guerre! I confess the deception which that monster practised upon
me for so long a time." Bertrande, also, who seems
to have been sometimes of one opinion, sometimes
of another during the trial, immediately admitted that
she had been deceived, and declared unhesitatingly
that the new-comer was her true husband. The two
men were placed side by side and compared. The
resemblance was astonishing; the old French reporter says : "Two eggs do not resemble each other
more than did these two men." But upon the new
testimony of the witnesses, now disavowing the
accused, the judges convicted him, and he was put to
death for his fraud. Before his death he made a
confession, saying that some intimate friends of
Martin Guerre, misled by the resemblance, had

accosted him by that name; which gave him the idea
of claiming Guerre's position and property; and that
he had gained his intimate knowledge of Guerre's
life partly from Guerre himself, whom he had known
slightly in the army, and partly from various acquaintances of Guerre.

There have been other very curious trials in which
the question has been to identify a person who
claimed to be some one else. There was once a
Marchioness de Douhault, who died, and was buried
with funeral services in the church, but three years
afterwards a lady came to the chateau, claiming to
be the Marchioness, and declaring that the funeral
was a fictitious one, and that she had been all the
while kept in an insane asylum by her wicked son, in
order that he might enjoy the property. She looked
so much like the Marchioness that at first she was
received with much rejoicing, but afterwards there
was a trial and the decision was against her. There
were several men, at various times, who pretended to
be Louis XVII., the dauphin of France, whose death
was officially announced in 1795, but was always
involved in mystery, and is a very interesting and

perplexing topic in the history of France; neither of them, however, met with any substantial success. There was once a man named Mège who pretended to be the son of a family named Caille; and a hundred and ten witnesses who had known the true Caille before he died, swore that Mège was he. One hundred and ninety-nine witnesses, however, testified to the contrary. These prevailed.

Only a few years ago, in New York City, a lady complained to the court that a brother of her dead husband had taken charge of his property and was managing it as his "administrator," but would not give her a proper share. The brother answered that the husband was not dead, but had authorized him to manage the property as he was doing; and he brought into the court room a man who declared himself to be the husband; but the wife, however, denied it very positively. Everybody was very much perplexed, and there was a long trial. But before it could be completed, the lady died.

The novels *Griffith Gaunt* and the *Missing Heir* are founded upon real trials where the question was 'who is who?" or a puzzle about personal identity.

VII.—DE BERENGER AND COCHRANE:
SWINDLING.

IN the days when the struggle between the great
Napoleon and the sovereigns who had allied to
conquer him was drawing towards a close, all England
was intensely anxious for the earliest news from the
seat of war. This anxiety was highest among business men in London, for the English government had
borrowed immense sums to be used in prosecuting
the war and would be made very poor by a defeat of
the allied armies.

The " stocks," or "funds," as the large investments
of money in England were called, would rise in price
very much if the allied armies should be victorious, or
fall greatly if Napoleon should conquer. But there
were no telegraphs then, and the newspapers were
small and feeble compared with those of our time ;
accordingly the Londoners, eager as they were for

intelligence, were dependent on such reports as might be brought by persons returning from the scene of the conflict.

Early one morning a stranger dressed in a peculiar military uniform arrived at a hotel in Dover (which is on the coast of the English Channel, opposite France), aroused the landlord and servants to give him some refreshments, and told them that he had just come from France, and that Napoleon had been defeated and killed in battle. From Dover he wrote letters announcing this news. He then travelled to London, spreading the intelligence; and soon after his arrival a postchaise drove through London streets carrying men dressed as French officers, wearing blue coats with white linings and white cockades, who, as they rode, threw from the windows of the chaise little pieces of paper telling the same story. At first people readily believed it; the "funds" rose rapidly in price, and speculators who bought early realized large profits. But very soon the story was found to be false. It was what is called a "hoax," ingeniously contrived to enable those speculators to make money. Napoleon was not dead, nor even defeated; and the pretended French stranger was a mere swindler.

The people who had lost money by the swindle naturally made an investigation. They ascertained that the stranger who brought the false news was named De Berenger; that when he arrived in London, he visited a Sir Thomas Cochrane, at the residence of the latter, and came away wearing a black coat and hat, instead of his French military attire; and that Sir Thomas and an uncle of his were among the persons who had made money by the hoax. These circumstances gave rise to a belief that Sir Thomas and his uncle had devised the plan, and had hired De Berenger to assist them, by starting from Dover as if he had just landed from France, and bringing the false news; and that De Berenger's visit to Sir Thomas was to enable the two to consult. Sir Thomas, his uncle, and De Berenger, with some other persons, were brought to trial for swindling, and were convicted. Sir Thomas was imprisoned for a year, fined a thousand pounds, expelled from the House of Commons, and otherwise disgraced. Thus we see that persons who can be clearly proved guilty of cheating or swindling are liable to severe punishment.

In this instance the proof, although it seemed clear at the time, was probably erroneous as to Lord Cochrane. He always denied having had anything to do with the swindle. When he was asked about the mysterious visit, he said that De Berenger came to him saying nothing about Napoleon, but complaining of being very poor and begging for aid in gaining some appointment or employment. When asked about De Berenger's change of dress at his house, he said that De Berenger borrowed the hat and coat from him in order to make a better appearance when calling on other people in search of business. When asked about the profit he made by the hoax, he showed that the business was managed by his broker, without his saying, doing, or knowing anything about it; moreover, that the profit realized was very little, and that he easily might have made five or ten times as much if he had been in the secret.

Gradually people became convinced that his story was true and that he had been unjustly condemned. He became very popular for this reason, though he was not a man of amiable or popular manners. His constituents re-elected him to Parliament. The common people made a great subscription of a penny for each person, to repay his one thousand pounds fine, and at last government formally restored him to the honors of which he had been deprived under the unjust verdict.

He became, in England, a rear-admiral, and also Earl Dundonald; and in South America, where he served several years after his troubles arising from the great hoax were over, he was appointed to high naval command, and was created Marquis of Maranhao.

I have read that a few years before his trial he fell in love with a beautiful young lady who was endeavoring to get an education, but was poor. He supplied money for her expenses at boarding-school, and afterwards was married to her; and although they were a contrast — " she young, sprightly, handsome, gay; he old, homely, stiff, serious " — they lived very affectionately and happily together for about forty years. He lived to be about eighty-five years old, and when he died, which was in 1860, he was honored by a burial in Westminster Abbey.

It may be that some of my readers will find some

information about swindling useful to protect them
from being cheated. There are, unhappily, many
persons scattered through the country who are busy in
contriving and practising swindles ; and a young person who has been educated to be honest and industrious is perhaps more liable on that very account to
be deceived ; for he does not imagine that people can
be so dishonest as sometimes they are. For example,
every one understands that merchants are accustomed
to advertise the goods they sell in the newspapers ;
and that a person living in a distant place can order
what he wishes to buy by means of a letter, and have
it sent to him by the express ; and that the expressman will receive the price and carry it back to the
merchant. A vast amount of honest buying and selling is done in this way. Swindlers take advantage of
the system in various ways. Sometimes they advertise watches or jewelry extraordinarily cheap, telling
some plausible reason why the price is so low. One
man advertised to sell a watch as good as ordinary
two-hundred-dollar watches for four dollars! saying
that he had the benefit of a new way of making gold,
just discovered. Sometimes they advertise a " gift

enterprise," or a " distribution " of piano-fortes, sew-ing-machines and other valuable articles among all who will purchase tickets.

Their plan is to send to you by express a parcel which looks as if it might contain whatever you wrote, for, directing the expressman to collect the price. When the expressman brings you the parcel, you will naturally give him the money; indeed he will not de-liver it without; and he will be gone before you will have time to examine your bargain. And you will find — if you are dealing with a swindler, not with an honest merchant — that the article inside is not worth half what you have paid, perhaps is not worth any-thing.

In one swindling trial the story was that a boy who bought a ticket in a gift enterprise received a notice that he had drawn a prize worth five hundred dollars, on which he was to pay twenty-five dollars. He borrowed the money and paid it to the expressman; but when he opened the parcel, behold! there was nothing within but old newspapers and sticks of wood. To get one's money back in such a case is usually impossible. The express sends it at once to the person from whom the parcel came; and he takes good care that the persons whom he has cheated shall not be able to find him. If, for instance, you send or go to the street number of his store, as given in his advertisement, you will learn that no such person has any store there; the swindler has some cunning arrangement for getting letters without being known.

Young men who visit the large cities in search of a business are often swindled by advertisements of a "Clerk wanted," or a "Business for sale." The swindler has a room fitted up with what appears to be a stock of goods, and gives a glowing account of his business and prospects. He wishes a cashier or a partner, but expects that the person whom he hires will deposit a few hundred dollars as security that he will do his work faithfully, or as part of the capital. Or he wishes to sell out on account of poor health, or because he has another store, and cannot manage both. But, if you give him the money, he will disappear and you will find the drawers, boxes and barrels have nothing in them of any value.

During the past ten years many persons have been

swindled by make-believe brokers who have advertised to take small sums of money and make great
profits on them by speculations in Wall street. Their
circulars described the best methods of speculating,
and offered to take small sums from anybody, lump
them in one large fund, speculate with it, and divide
profits with those who contributed. They even
promised to guarantee that there should not be any
losses!

But if you send money in answer to such offers, no
profit will come. When you write asking questions
no answer at all will be returned, or you will receive
a letter explaining that by reason of very extraordinary circumstances there was a loss in the particular
speculation; but you had better try again, as it is
impossible there should be a loss the second time.
Usually the make-believe broker sends this sort of
answer to his dissatisfied customers as long as he can
persuade them to wait, but when they complain to
the police, and the officers search for him, he changes
his name and removes to another city.

To speculate in Wall street in any way is dangerous; to send money to brokers who advertise to

guarantee that it will not be lost, is simply throwing it away. What are called "confidence men" have very ingenious ways of cultivating acquaintance with strangers, winning their confidence, and imposing upon them by some plausible story.

There is an account of a wealthy American who was invited by a very pleasant, gentlemanly man whom he met to take dinner at a restaurant. The gentlemanly stranger affected not to understand French very well, and became involved in a discussion with the waiter about the bill; whereupon another gentlemanly man, overhearing the trouble, drew near, volunteered to assist, and by his better knowledge of the language, settled the difficulty pleasantly. This led to a conversation in which the new-comer said that he had inherited from a relative who was very fond of the Americans, a large estate, on the condition that he should send twenty thousand dollars to be distributed among the poor in this country. Swindler No. 1 suggested that the gentleman whom he had brought to dine with him was an American and would perhaps take charge of the money. Swindler No. 2 said he should be happy to make that

arrangement if the American gentleman could exhibit a corresponding sum to show that he was
respectable and trustworthy.

And the American was actually induced by this
story to come the next day, bringing several thousand
dollars in bank notes to prove that he deserved to be
entrusted with the twenty thousand dollars. The
swindlers easily contrived to get it into their hands
and ran away with it. In large cities, and in travelling, it is very difficult to know how to avoid persons
who are trying to make acquaintance for the purpose
of cheating, while you are courteous and kindly
towards honest and respectable strangers. Perhaps
the best protection against such swindles as I have
described is to be really honest and industrious ; to
be ambitious of earning your money by genuine work,
and willing to pay a fair price for whatever you
buy.

If the American traveller in Paris had not desired
to get twenty thousand dollars for nothing ; if the
customers of the advertising brokers had not wished
to get profits of speculation without running any corresponding risk ; if the boy who subscribed to the

gift enterprise had not hoped to get five hundred dollars' worth for only twenty-five dollars, the devices of the swindlers would not have attracted them, and they would have saved their money.

VIII. — ANDRE AND MACKENZIE: COURTS MARTIAL.

WHEN persons in ordinary civil society are to be tried for a crime, it is considered very important to give them a trial by jury. A "jury" consists of twelve men chosen by lot from the reputable, trustworthy residents of the part of the country where the offence was committed. The twelve hear the witnesses and lawyers' speeches, the judge explains to them the law, and they are then shut in a room by themselves, where they discuss what has been said, and vote. Whenever all are agreed to say "guilty" or "not guilty," they return to the court-room, and the chief juror or "foreman" announces the decision. There are very strict laws for securing to every accused person a trial by jury, and for making sure that the jurors are honest and impartial.

That the jurors should be the social equals of the

accused has always been deemed a valuable element in the privilege of trial by jury. In England, where people are classed as "lords" or "commoners," if a lord is charged with an offence, he is not tried by a jury of commoners, but by the House of Lords; for the saying is, that every one has the right to be tried by his peers; that is, by his equals. In America there are no lords; a Senator or Representative may be tried by his neighbors, for the saying in this country is, that "all men are born equal." Yet there have been some laws that a foreigner or that a negro should have the right to have some persons of his own country or race summoned on a jury which is to try him, in order that the trial may be by his equals.

It is interesting to know that trials in the army or navy are conducted on the opposite principle. A soldier or sailor is not tried by his equals, but by his superiors in rank. Why there is this difference would be hard to explain. One would think that if trial by a jury of equals chosen by lot were a natural, valuable right, soldiers and sailors should enjoy it; but they do not. Probably the army and navy could not be managed with efficiency if the officers were obliged to submit every charge of disobedience of orders, mu'iny and other offences to the decision of some of the equals of the accused. Therefore military and naval trials are by " court-martial ; " that is, by a board of officers not chosen by lot, but appointed by the commanding general; and usually of higher rank in the service than the accused person. In time of war persons who are not soldiers are often tried in the military manner, instead of by a jury.

To illustrate this difference, I shall give a brief account of a military and a naval trial. Every reader knows the story of Major André. When Benedict Arnold, during the Revolutionary War, was planning his treasonable surrender of West Point to Clinton, the English general, the latter sent Major André to Arnold to discuss arrangements and bring papers; and he was caught while on his return, going in a false name, wearing a disguise, and carrying the papers hidden in his boots. These circumstances made him a spy. It is not considered necessary in war to give a spy a formal trial, therefore André's fate might lawfully have been decided by General Washington alone. But Washington chose to order

a military trial. Instead of choosing a jury by lot
from among people living in the neighborhood of
West Point, and thus, perhaps, drawing several
Tories who would have been sure to vote "not
guilty," he selected army officers, six major-generals,
one of whom was the famous Marquis de Lafayette,
and eight brigadier-generals. Besides these there
was, as there always is in a court-martial, a "judge-
advocate," whose duty it is to conduct the prosecu-
tion, and explain the law to the other members of the
court. The name of the judge-advocate in the trial
of André was John Lawrence. This board of fifteen
officers assembled at Tappan in New York. André
was brought before them, was shown the letters and
papers which had been taken from him, and was
asked what explanation or defence he had to give.
His story was heard, but it amounted to a confession
that he had come within the American lines secretly
and in disguise to obtain information for the British
general; and the board reported to General Washington that by the laws of war he should be hung as a
spy.

A trial of another man by court-martial followed—

was commenced on the next day after the examination of André. The accused was a lawyer living in the neighborhood of West Point, who was accused of having assisted Arnold in his interviews and arrangements with André. The court was composed of a colonel, a lieutenant-colonel, a major, and nine captains, with John Lawrence again as judge-advocate. On André's trial it seems not to have been thought needful to call witnesses as he did not deny the facts; but upon Smith's trial many witnesses were examined, among them two of the men by whom André was captured, who gave a minute account of the circumstances of the arrest. These witnesses clearly proved that Mr. Smith had rendered Arnold considerable assistance, that he accompanied Arnold on one or two of his expeditions to negotiate with Clinton, that Arnold and André were at Smith's house conferring together, one night, that Smith furnished André with the suit of clothes he wore as a disguise, and aided him in starting on his way back, and similar matters. But the board doubted whether Smith knew, at the time, that Arnold was plotting treason; he might, they thought, have supposed he was obeying lawful orders and assisting Arnold in the performance of duty; therefore they acquitted him.

Two remarkable naval trials arose out of the misconduct of a midshipman named Philip Spencer, on board the brig *Somers*, in 1842. The commander of the vessel was named Mackenzie. He learned from Wales, the purser's steward on board the ship, that Spencer was plotting a mutiny. Wales' story was that Spencer had told him that about twenty of the crew had agreed to seize the vessel, kill Commander Mackenzie and other officers, and sail the ship as a pirate; and had asked him to join. Spencer had also said that he had a. memorandum in secret writing of all the details of the plan, and of the names of those who were in the secret. They intended, he said, as soon all was ready, to start a make-believe fight among themselves upon deck, and the officers, when they interfered, would be seized and thrown overboard. Upon hearing this disclosure, with many particulars, Commander Mackenzie directed that Midshipman Spencer should be arrested, which was done. The culprit's "locker" was then searched, and in his razor case were found papers written in Greek characters, which appeared to contain lists of names such as Spencer had described to Wales.

For two or three days after the arrest, the Commander kept Spencer in confinement, hoping to be able to carry him to port for trial; but at length he became suspicious that the other mutineers were proceeding with the plan. He arrested two more, and put the three in irons; but this did not seem to quiet the difficulty. Indications of an intended mutiny increased, and the commander became satisfied that his vessel was in danger. He decided to have such a trial as he could under the circumstances. If he had selected jurors by lot, probably several of the mutineers would have been drawn, and, of course, they would have voted "not guilty." He called a council of seven officers and midshipmen whom he knew he could trust, laid all the facts before them, and asked their advice. They heard the stories of Wales and some others, examined the Greek documents, and decided that the prisoners had been guilty of plotting a dangerous mutiny, and that the safety of the ship and of the innocent persons on board demanded that they should be put to death.   Accordingly they were, during the same day, hung.

'This trial, like the examination of André, was not strictly a court-martial, for both Washington and Mackenzie acted, finally, on their own judgment and responsibility, the councils being called only to advise them.   But when Commander Mackenzie's vessel reached home, he was tried before a formal court-martial on the accusation of having committed murder by hanging the three prisoners.   His council argued that there were strong reasons for believing that a mutiny was in progress, and the vessel and the lives of those on board were in danger; and that when such is the case, a commander, if he cannot safely carry the offenders home, may put them to death.   The judge-advocate contended that as no one had actually done anything mutinous, the commander should have been more patient : that he was bound to endeavor to carry the prisoners home. The court decided in the commander's favor.   Probably the fact that the members of the court were all officers in the navy, would have some tendency to cause such a decision.

IX.—ELIZABETH CANNING: DIRECT TESTIMONY.

IN a previous chapter I narrated some trials illustrating the danger of trusting to Circumstantial Evidence. This month's article will show that Direct Testimony is often untrustworthy.

The trial of Elizabeth Canning is a famous example. About a hundred and thirty years ago Elizabeth, then a girl of eighteen, was employed as a domestic in an English family. One New Year's day she asked leave to spend the holiday with her uncle; her mistress consented, and she went. Night came, and days followed, but she did not return. It was meantime ascertained that she made the intended visit at her uncle's and that her uncle and aunt accompanied her part of the way back in the evening; but beyond this no trace of her could be discovered until the very end of January, when she appeared at her mother's house, emaciated, pale, weak, evidently almost starved, scarcely clothed, and showing a recent wound upon her ear. "Why, Elizabeth! where have you been? What has happened?" and many like questions were poured upon her. Her story was — and the reader should understand that she had always borne a high character as a blameless, trustworthy girl — that, after parting from her uncle and aunt on New Year's night, she proceeded towards her employer's home, when she was attacked by two men who robbed her of what money she had, stripped off her gown, and dragged her along the road for some distance, to a house into which they carried her. Here she was taken in charge of by a "tall and swarthy" old woman whom she thought she heard called "Mother Wells!" This woman shut her up in a "longish, darkish" room, which Elizabeth described particularly, and here she was kept confined with scarcely any food, until the day of her return home, when she contrived to escape through the window; but in so doing tore her ear.

There was some little corroboration of her story; and there was a house in the neighborhood she described,

kept by a landlady named Wells; therefore the
police carried Elizabeth to this house, and here she
showed them the room in which she said she had
been confined, and pointed out the board nailed
against the window against which she declared she
hurt her ear.

The police then collected the inmates of the house
in one room and asked Elizabeth if she could identify
the woman who had kept her imprisoned ; but instead
of designating " Mother Wells," she pointed to an old
gypsy woman sitting by the fire, and said " That old
woman in the corner was the woman who robbed
me."

Then began the conflict of Direct Testimony. The
gypsy arose from her seat, threw aside a cloak which
had partly concealed her face, looked steadily at
Elizabeth, and exclaimed, solemnly : " Me rob you !
I never saw you in my life, before. For God
Almighty's sake, do not swear my life away ! Pray,
madam, look at me in the face; if you have once
seen it before you must have remembered it," etc.
And, sure enough, it was a face which could not well
be mistaken for another ; being naturally very ugly,

and also deeply scarred. But Elizabeth adhered to her story.

"Pray, madam," said the gypsy, "when do you say I robbed you?"

"On New Year's day," answered Elizabeth.

"Lord bless me!" exclaimed the gypsy; "I was a hundred and twenty miles from this place then." And the gypsy's son who was present declared the same. But Elizabeth's story was so far believed that the gypsy and some other persons residing in the house, were brought to trial for imprisoning and mal-treating Elizabeth, and, chiefly on her testimony, were convicted. The gypsy called several witnesses who testified that on the New Year's day they saw her at places far away; but they were disbelieved. But the judge doubted the correctness of the verdict. And many persons shared his doubts. Soon the case gave rise to great discussion throughout London. No less than three dozen pamphlets were issued, some espousing Elizabeth Canning's case, some taking sides with the gypsy. The famous novelist, Fielding, who was a London magistrate at the time, and had taken some of the testimony, wrote in favor of the verdict; and the painter Ramsay contended against it. There was a new and more thorough investigation, the result of which was that Elizabeth was put upon trial in her turn, for having sworn falsely against the gypsy.

On this trial so many more witnesses came forward to prove that the gypsy was in quite another part of England on the New Year's day, that the jury, though doubtingly and reluctantly, found Elizabeth guilty. She was sentenced to be transported to New England, which was a punishment sometimes used in those days — it would not be deemed a very severe one now! But there were many people who believed her to have been unjustly condemned, and a considerable sum of money was subscribed and given to her to make her exile comfortable. And to this day it is regarded as very uncertain whether her story of her long absence and of the gypsy's cruelty to her was true or false. On the one hand: what possible motive could she have for making up such a story, or how could she be mistaken about such a remarkable countenance? On the other hand: how could so many honest witnesses be mistaken in declaring that the gypsy was in their part of the country at the time ? The truth will never be known.

The truth of this particular case is no longer of any importance, but it is important that young persons should realize how difficult it is to depend even on Direct Testimony. Lawyers very early learn that if circumstances often deceive, so also witnesses are frequently untrustworthy. Lying witnesses are not the only ones who mislead. Every one knows that persons do sometimes come into court intending to swear to a fictitious story. This is the crime of perjury; and it is severely punished whenever it can be detected and proved. Just as Elizabeth Canning was transported for the perjury which the jury thought she had committed, so at the present day, any one who can be proved to have committed it, is sent to prison. But mistaken witnesses create even more difficulty than dishonest ones. And not only in lawsuits, but also in daily life every one needs to remember that it is not safe to depend too confidingly upon what is told us, even when the speakers mean to tell the truth.

There are several causes which embarrass persons

in narrating what they have seen, and therefore throw some doubt over all Direct Testimony. One is the great difference in the perceptive powers. One person can see very distinctly but does not hear well; he will give a correct account of things visible, but he may err very much as to what was said in his presence! yet may be unaware of the trouble. Another can hear perfectly, but is near-sighted; he will be a good witness as to what was said, but not as to the appearance of things. Clouds or sunshine, fog or clear weather, noises in the neighborhood, haste and inattention, and various like causes make more difference than many persons know, in their power of perceiving accurately what is happening around them. One is often sure that a thing did not occur, because if it had he must have perceived it, when in fact it did occur, but he did not notice it.

Forgetfulness prevents persons from giving accurate accounts; especially of what was said. Few can remember minutely the words of even a brief conversation. Whenever any one repeats the language of another, it is safest to remember that very likely the repetition is not accurate; something may have been forgotten and omitted which would quite change the sense; yet the witness may honestly suppose he is relating the matter correctly. And this fact is very curious, that many minds will mistake an imagination of incidents for a memory of them. In recalling an event which took place a while ago, fancy suggests details which cluster around the principal fact, and seem really to have been parts of it; and the person at length mistakes the images suggested by fancy for realities restored by memory. This is a fertile cause, not generally understood, of the errors which creep into Direct Testimony.

Illusions may sometimes wholly deceive a person as to what he has seen or heard. These do not occur very often, but there is abundant evidence that they do occur, and it is often possible that a person who is relating something which he sincerely believes occurred in his presence, is, in reality, only describing an illusion of the senses.

When either of these causes of error coöperate with a bias or wish in the mind of the witness, his narrative is almost sure te be perverted from the truth.

Suppose a person who dislikes another very much, is relating something which the other has done; the dislike will greatly increase the probability that details will be varied to the other's disadvantage.

Suppose, on the contrary, one is narrating matters about a very dear friend; the sentiment of affection will tend to weaken recollection of unfavorable details, and stimulate imagination of commendatory incidents; and the result will be a version which, though honest in intention, is quite erroneous.

In all the affairs of life, whenever we are called upon to depend upon the accounts given us by other persons, we need to consider carefully their powers of sense, of memory and of fancy, and their sentiments or wishes, and to make allowance for there being powerful causes of error in these various fields. Especially is this important when unfavorable stories are brought to us about our friends and neighbors. Though the story-teller may be honest, there are many ways in which he may be mistaken. It is not best to form harsh judgments of the absent, even upon Direct Testimony which appears perfectly honest and convincing. Wait and hear the other side.

X.—TRIAL OF MADAME RACHEL: SPURI-
OUS COSMETICS.

THE Rachel whose trial I am to narrate is not the famous actress of that name, but a noto-rious cheat who lived in London about fifteen years ago. Her original name was Russell, but after her marriage her full name was Sarah Rachel Leverson, and she used the middle name "Rachel" in her business of selling perfumery and cosmetics. The story is that in early life she had unusually long and beautiful hair, but in a severe fever the doctor who attended her was obliged to order her head shaved; he, however, gave her a recipe for a prep-aration which he said would make it grow again. She recovered from the illness, and applied the preparation, when, sure enough, the hair grew won-derfully fast and long, owing, perhaps, to the virtue of the prescription, but more probably because of its natural vigor. However, she commenced making the article for sale, and advertising that she would restore the color of gray hair. Soon she added other articles to her stock in trade, and in time established an extensive business.

The law does not forbid making or selling cosmetics in an honest way, but it does forbid a dealer's cheating customers by spurious articles and false advertisements; and this is what Madame Rachel was at length tempted into doing. She published a pamphlet entitled *Beautiful For Ever*, describing a great many washes and powders for making the elderly look young, and the plain handsome. There were the "Circassian Beauty Wash," the "Magnetic Rock Dew Water of Sahara," for removing wrinkles (remember that Sahara is a sandy desert), the Alabaster Liquid," the "Youth and Beauty Bloom," the "Medicated Cream," for rendering the hair black or chestnut brown, the "Royal Arabian Toilet of Beauty," arranged for the Sultana of Turkey and various European royal brides, price one thousand guineas, and ever so many more. Above all was the secret, costly process of "enamelling" the countenance,

whereby it could be preserved from all the changes
of life, and literally be kept "Beautiful for ever."
No doubt many persons were cheated into buying
these nostrums, but one who suffered severely was a
Mrs. Borradaile. She was a widow, elderly, credu-
lous, and worth about £5000. She became a customer at Madame Rachel's store, and Madame
Rachel asked her why she did not have her face
enamelled and be made "Beautiful for ever." She
asked, "What would be the cost?" Madame Rachel
said, "A thousand pounds." Mrs. Borradaile hesi-
tated about paying so much, and, to persuade her,
Madame Rachel told her a story of a nobleman
named Lord Ranelagh who had seen her and fallen
in love with her, and was very desirous of marrying
her if only she were a little handsomer. She even
introduced her to some one who called himself Lord
Ranelagh, but it is not certainly known who or what
he was. However, Mrs. Borradaile decided to be
"enamelled." Then began the "treatment." There
were baths, and washes, and powders, but no improvement in beauty. However, the process was
continued as long as the customer's money lasted.

She paid Madame Rachel one sum after another
until her little fortune of £5000 was gone, and ran
in debt to her, beyond, yet did not grow beautiful.
At length she realized that she had been, as she
herself expressed it, "a lunatic." She made a complaint against Madame Rachel, who was tried for
"obtaining money by false pretences," and was
found guilty and sentenced to five years' imprisonment.

To illustrate how ingenious the dealer was and
how easily the customer was deceived, I may men-
tion that while the cheat was proceeding, Madame
Rachel brought to Mrs. Borradaile several love-let-
ters, one after another, which she said had been
written and sent by "Lord Ranelagh." They contained many mistakes of spelling, and Mrs. Borradaile expressed surprise that a nobleman should
spell so badly. Madame Rachel explained that
Lord Ranelagh had sprained his arm, and was
obliged to employ an amanuensis, and the person
employed was uneducated! This seemed perfectly
satisfactory to the deluded widow.

American newspapers are full of glowing advertisements promising all kinds of benefit from various cosmetics and toilet preparations. Many of these articles, no doubt, have some merit, but in respect to several, when lawsuits over them have arisen, and the manufacturers and dealers have been summoned to tell in court how what they sold was made, they have been obliged to confess that the thing was a cheat and the advertisement a lie. In one instance a dealer began making and selling a toilet-water which he called " Balm of Thousand Flowers." It sold so well, that soon a rival dealer put forth a similar one called " Balm of Ten Thousand Flowers." The first dealer complained to the court that the second was imitating his goods and advertisements and so taking away his business. The court asked him what his " Balm " was, and what were the " Flowers " contained. He said that it was composed in part of honey, and that as the bees in gathering honey suck from every kind of flower in a large circle of country, he considered that his article was very truthfully called " Balm of Thousand Flowers ! " When the judge heard this he declared he would have nothing to do with aiding or protecting either " Balm." He said that a dealer who is himself imposing upon the public has no right to complain of another for doing the same.

There was a similar lawsuit over a cosmetic which was advertised over the name of Fabian & Co., of London, as, "Meen Fun," the celebrated Chinese skin powder for restoring, beautifying and preserving the complexion, patronized by her Majesty, the Queen. On the trial it was found that the article was not made in London, but in New York, and that Queen Victoria had probably never even heard of it. The dealers pleaded that it was the prevailing belief in this country (this was said about twenty-five years ago) that ladies' toilet articles of English or French manufacture were superior to any American, and they excused themselves on this ground for making the false statement of their label. But the judge decided that they were deceiving the public, and therefore could not have the aid or protection of his court. There was also the "Gouraud Oriental Cream" case. The original name of the inventor was Trust; but he adopted the name "Dr. Gouraud" for his sign, advertisements and labels, and

became so well known under this name that at
length he had his name legally changed from Trust
to Gouraud. His sons, however, kept the old name.
Years afterwards they introduced an Oriental Cream,
which they sold under the name Dr. Gouraud's
Sons. Their father complained of this to the court.
The sons said: "We are Dr. Gouraud's sons, therefore our label is perfectly true." But the court said
that they were using the label for the purpose of mis-
leading buyers of their Cream to suppose that it was
the father's original preparation which they sold;
and that this must be stopped.

Advertisements of medicines abound in the newspapers, and circulars boasting of the beneficial effect of some remedy and describing wonderful cures
it has wrought are constantly appearing. To make
and sell these medicines and advertise them thus is
not unlawful, and even if the advertisement somewhat exaggerates the merit of the pills or potions
which it describes, or promises more than they will
or can perform, the dealer cannot be sued for this.
The law considers that the public should exercise
reasonable care and common sense, and ought not to

believe all that advertisements say. When, however, there is any downright falsehood or cheating — when a person is induced to buy the article by gross deception which his using common sense or making proper inquiry would not enable him to detect, the merchant can be prosecuted. Even labeling a medicine falsely, by accident or mistake, may give rise to a lawsuit. There was once a lady who was taken violently sick, and nearly died, after taking some medicine which the apothecary of the village had sent to her as " extract of dandelion." The doctors and lawyers examined what was left in the phial and found it to contain belladonna, which is a violent poison. They inquired of the apothecary and found that he had filled the prescription from a jar labelled Extract of Dandelion, which he purchased from a manufacturing druggist. Therefore he was not to blame. They then inquired of the manufacturer and learned that by some mistake in labelling the jars, some containing belladonna had been sent over the country by mistake for jars of dandelion. They then brought suit. The unfortunate manufacturer said it was an accident; they meant to label the jars correctly and had no intention of selling a poison. But the court said that to mean well is not enough in selling dangerous medicines; dealers are bound to label them correctly. And the lady recovered $800, to pay her for having been made so ill. The stories of these various lawsuits, if one were to read them, would show very plainly that there are many mistakes and a great deal of exaggeration, deception and cheating in making and selling cosmetics and medicines, and that those persons are wisest who remain contented with their natural hair and complexions, and seek health by good diet and exercise, or by the advice and prescriptions of a trustworthy physician. Whoever trusts to advertisements in these matters will be likely to say, some day, with Mrs. Borradaile: " I think I must have been a lunatic."

XI.— TRIAL OF HOPLEY: CRUELTY TO CHILDREN.

THE question has always been perplexing how far police officers and judges ought to interfere with the management of children. The parents seem to be the proper persons to take care of children, and they usually have a natural instinct of affection which restrains from cruelty and neglect. Next to the parents are the teachers to whose care children are intrusted by their parents; and they are subject to the general directions which the parents give. Formerly it was thought best to leave the care of children almost wholly to their parents and teachers. But some have no parents; some are too poor to go to school; some parents and teachers have shown themselves to be careless or even unkind, hence laws have been passed to make better provision for their safety and education.

There was once in England a schoolmaster named Hopley, who had in his school a boy who was dull, and seemed to the master to be obstinate in neglecting his lessons. The master whipped the pupil once or twice, but this produced no change; and he then wrote to the father, saying : " If the boy were my son I should subdue his obstinacy by chastising him severely, and if necessary, should do it again and again." The father answered : " I do not wish to interfere with your plan." The teacher then chastised the boy for about two hours so severely that the lad died the next morning. Of course, for such cruelty as this, the teacher was tried. His lawyer argued that punishing disobedient pupils in school is lawful; but the judge said that only a moderate punishment is lawful, and a moderate one would never cause death. The fact that the father consented was urged in defence; but the judge said that a father cannot give or authorize an excessive chastisement. The lawyer argued that the teacher believed that the lad was obstinate, and that he himself was only doing his duty. But the judge said that his mistaken motive was no defense for using excessive and dangerous violence. So the teacher was found guilty.

A very similar instance occurred about seventy-five years ago in New York State. The unfortunate pupil was a little girl of about six years. She could not or would not pronounce properly some of the words given out in the spelling-class and particularly she pronounced the word "gig" as if it were spelled "jig." The teacher thought that she refused obstinately, and he began punishing her to compel her, to say the word aright. The truth probably was that she did not know the correct sound, or perhaps she could not make it; therefore he continued the punishment so severely and long that the child died a few days afterward. He was found guilty of murder.

In Bengal there was once employed in the school of the English missionaries a schoolmaster named John MacRay who had two daughters. When his wife, their mother, died, his sister Helen became his housekeeper, and took charge of the girls. She was morbidly strict and severe in her ideas of how children should behave and of her duty in managing her little nieces. One would have supposed that as the girls grew older the rigor of the aunt's discipline might have relaxed, but instead of this her treatment of them became more and more severe; their food was reduced to a mere porridge, their lessons and tasks were made excessively onerous, and the punishments inflicted for any fault or failure were even cruel. At length the youngest girl, exhausted with hunger, probably, was detected in stealing, as her aunt considered it, some preserves. The aunt thought what the child said when reproved was impertinent, and commenced to punish her. She probably acted from a certain morbid sense of duty, at any rate there was no concealment; she even sent for the father to come in from his school. He remonstrated, but lacked courage to oppose his sister's imperious will, and she continued the punishment until the little girl died. Both aunt and father were brought to trial. The only defense which could be made for them seems to be that parents have a right to chastise refractory children and that if they act sincerely in doing so they are chargeable only with error of judgment, not with a crime. But they were found guilty, and sentenced to be transported for life.

In different parts of this country there have been

a number of trials of schoolteachers for harsh treatment of pupils, and the judges have said that moderate punishment for serious misconduct is lawful, but if the twelve men who are called to try a teacher feel sure that the punishment he inflicted was unreasonably severe, he may be sent to prison. This may be done either when the pupil has been punished without having done anything very wrong or without being told what his fault was, or when the punishment has been barbarous in manner or too long continued.

Such trials as these have shown, I think, that some parents and teachers who suppose they have authority to punish children in order to make them do right, are mistaken. A child may be punished (moderately) for having done wrong, and this probably will gradually teach him to do right. But undertaking to punish for the purpose of compelling a child to do what has been commanded — to recite a lesson, put playthings away, to confess a fault, or the like, — is a different and sometimes a dangerous thing, and is probably unlawful. At any rate, such trials have shown that there was need of stricter laws for protecting children from cruelty, not only in punishments, but in others things. And many have been passed within a few years. Some such laws require parents and guardians to send their children to school for at least some weeks in every year, so that the little things shall not grow up without at least a partial education. Others forbid managers of mines or factories from employing children who are under a certain age, or for more than a certain length of time daily, or at tasks which are deemed too hard or dangerous for their tender frames. Likewise, in some places, recent laws forbid that children should be employed to sing or dance in public exhibitions, or should engage in dangerous performances such as walking a tight-rope or riding swift horses in a theatre or circus. Then there are laws by which little children who are cruelly treated by their parents or guardians or have been deserted by those who ought to take care of them, may be taken in charge by police officers and carried to asylums to be fed, clothed and educated. And in some cities where friendless children are numerous, benevolent societies have been organized to care for them and insist on the laws for their protection being obeyed.

Some time since I gave you an account of the case of little Louis Victor who was rescued by such a society from a sort of asylum where he was slowly starving. In a great variety of such cases where persons who have the charge of a child are neglecting or abusing it and the child is actually suffering, a society, or any benevolent person willing to make a complaint, can almost always, under modern laws, secure relief and protection.

Is it unlawful to employ children to dance and sing, act parts in plays or perform in circuses and exhibitions? There are many shows and performances in which there are parts particularly appropriate for children. Suppose, for instance, there were to be an exhibition of Dombey and Son, or of the Old Curiosity Shop; how could the parts of Paul and Florence or Little Nell be filled by grown persons? Many persons think that if the children employed in these plays and exhibitions are comfortable and happy, if they are willing to perform and satisfied with the treatment and wages they receive, there is no cruelty, and the judges and police officers ought not to interfere. " Children," they say, "have a right to work in ways which they like and their parents approve, to earn their living." The benevolent persons who have formed the societies say that little children are not able to judge what employments are safe for them; that exhibitions which keep them up late at night, require unusual and dangerous exertions, and involve them in the excitements of appearing in public, are unwholesome, and are not less so because the child may enjoy the excitement and be pleased with the idea of earning wages. Also they point out that children who are kept busily engaged in rehearsals and practice and in evening performances, cannot have time and strength for attending school and acquiring a proper education; and they have gathered testimony of many physicians who say that such employments are dangerous to the health of young children, and of some experienced and successful managers of public entertainments who say that the effect of allowing young children to take part in such performances, even as much as they sometimes like to do, is harmful in other respects. In New York, within a year or two past, there have been several trials to determine whether young people should be allowed to perform in public or whether they should be kept at home or in school until older.

ALL my readers of course know the general story of the famous French heroine of the fifteenth century, and have heard the familiar conundrum : *What was Joan of Arc made of ? Ans. Maid of Orleans.* They have read how she grew up a plain and untaught country girl, during a time of quarrels and wars: how she came to believe that she saw visions of the Virgin and Saints, and heard voices commanding that she should go to the assistance of the king; how she volunteered to lead the army, and served so bravely and successfully that the enemies of King Charles the Seventh were routed, and he was crowned, and was established on the throne ; and, how in a later battle she was taken captive, and was afterwards tried, condemned and burned. They will, perhaps, like to know how it could be that so patriotic, useful, yet modest and innocent a young woman as she is described should be put to death as a criminal.

To ascertain the exact truth about matters which occurred so long ago, is not easy. The name usually given to the heroine, " D'Arc " (written as if she were of noble family), is probably a mistake; the true name is said to be Darc (in one word), and her parents were poor country people. There has been dispute whether she accomplished, in military affairs, anything more than to arouse the enthusiasm of the romantic French soldiers by the idea that a young and lovely woman, divinely inspired, was their general. One learned man has even doubted whether she was really put to death ; he thinks another person was deceptively burned in her stead. But accounts of her trial have been preserved which are quite explicit.

Jeanne Darc, or Joan of Arc, was taken by French and English troops who were fighting as allies against King Charles the Seventh of France, and his forces. She seems to have been sold, as it were, by one military captain to another, and was held awhile at Rouen as an English captive ; but ere long a demand came from France that she should be tried for witchcraft.

The king of England — very disgracefully, according
to modern views — consented. Why that king of
France, whom Jeanne had so signally assisted, did
not interpose to protect her, is not easy to see;
perhaps he lacked moral courage; possibly he shared
the belief in witchcraft, then very prevalent, so fully
as to think that even assisting him to attain the
throne was criminal if done by sorcery. Probably a
sovereign or general of the present day would repu-
diate any person who should attempt to aid him in
gaining victory by means of secretly poisoning the
food or water of the opposite army, and would allow
such person to be tried for the poisoning, notwithstanding the motive for it; and King Charles may
have regarded the charge that Jeanne had used magic
arts in his behalf, in somewhat the same way. Then
again the trial was not had in a court of law, or before
the King's judges, but was conducted before eccle-
siastics, the officers of the Inquisition, the chief
manager being the bishop of Beauvois. The accusation was a document long enough to fill several pages
of this book. It charged Jeanne with having
avowed that various saints — Gabriel, Michael, and

many others — had visited her from time to time, bringing commands and revelations from God, such as the order to volunteer to command the army, also to assume man's clothing, under which commands she had performed her military acts. According to the custom of the time, she was very harshly and unjustly interrogated by her judges, who used all ingenuity and severity to entangle her in contradictions or admissions. At length they announced their decision that she had invented the apparitions and revelations, that she was a superstitious sorceress, and that she must recant and submit to the Church, else she should be burned. According to accounts of the trial they deceived her in various ways. Thus when she was urged to submit to the Church, she expressed a willingness to do so, and the judges wrote a short and simple paper of submission, which they read over to her. But she could not read or write; and when the time for signing it came, they cunningly substituted a long confession of a great variety of misconduct, which she signed, supposing it to be the brief submission which she had heard. This paper included an admission of guiltiness in wearing man's clothing and armor, and a pledge that she would no longer do so. She signed it without really knowing what it contained. Soon after her jailers, at night, took away her woman's clothing and left in its place her masculine apparel, and she, having nothing else to wear, and not understanding the trick intended, put on the latter. The judges then called her to account for having broken her written pledge. She defended herself forcibly and touchingly; but as her condemnation had been determined, all she could say was of course useless. She was sentenced to be burned, and this cruel sentence was carried into effect.

The absurd and superstitious folly of trying and executing people for witchcraft was not confined to France. The idea as to witchcraft seems to have been that a person could, by making some bargain with evil spirits, obtain supernatural powers of doing mischief of various kinds; accordingly any one who had a mysterious illness or suffered any trouble which he or she could not understand, was apt to complain of some neighbor as a witch, and the charge was, of course, almost impossible to be disproved. For about a hundred and fifty years in

England there were occasional trials for witchcraft.
One famous case occurred before Lord Chief Justice
Hale, who was in other matters a very learned, wise
and humane judge, but who shared the common delusion as to witches. Two widow women, named Rose
Cullender and Amy Duny, were brought to trial
before him for bewitching children. Very absurd
stories were related by the witnesses. One was that
Amy Duny, in the form of a toad, had haunted one of
the children, but the mother by order of a witch
doctor had cast the toad into the fire, upon which it
exploded like gunpowder, and next day Amy Duny
was found to be very badly burned. Another was
that by their magical arts the witches had filled the
bodies of some of the children with crooked pins.
There were other charges of their having made the
children sick, lame, dumb, etc. Chief Justice Hale
told the jury that undoubtedly there were such things
as witches, and that they had only to consider
whether these children had been bewitched, and
whether the prisoners were guilty of it. The jury
found them all guilty. Next morning the children
came to Judge Hale's house, all quite recovered,

and they declared that they began to recover just after the verdict of guilty was rendered. This, which people nowadays would consider strong evidence that the children were either under an extraordinary delusion, or else were parties to a cheat and conspiracy, was deemed by the judge a reason for believing that the verdict was a just one. And the two unfortunate women were hung a few days afterward.

There were many similar trials, and historians have estimated that about thirty thousand persons suffered death in England on charges of this kind during about a century and a half. At one time an officer was appointed called the " Witchfinder." His method was to cast the suspected witch into a river or pond. If she sank, he pronounced her innocent; she was, however, usually drowned. If she floated, he declared her a witch, and she was put to death. In Scotland, also, there were many of those trials, and a number of poor friendless creatures suffered death under the same superstitious belief. Neighbors who had mysterious diseases, or whose cattle died, or whose crops failed, or who had other calamities, could think of no better solution than that some decrepit, homely, friendless old woman was bewitching them; and to detect the witch and put her to death was supposed to be a cure for the troubles, whatever they were. It is lamentable to think that the same cruel superstition prevailed for a short time in this country — even in Massachusetts.

The early settlers who came from England during the time when the belief in witchcraft prevailed, brought it with them, and, about 1688, a great excitement on the subject arose, which continued for several years. In an early and noted case some children named Goodwin were believed to have been bewitched, and a poor, half-crazy Irish woman was tried and executed for the offence. The excitement spread until at length, in one year, twenty supposed witches were executed (one of whom was a clergyman), and as many as three hundred and fifty persons stood accused.

Educated people, especially lawyers and judges, now understand that there is not really any such thing as witchcraft; that is to say, there is no way

possible of making compacts with evil spirits to obtain supernatural power of doing mischief, and no
one could now be tried as a witch, though persons
are sometimes tried for cheating by pretending to be
possessed of magical powers, and obtaining money
by professing to tell fortunes, recover lost money and
the like by magic arts. What, then, are the uses of
knowing about witchcraft? One is to enable us to
instruct uneducated people, of whom there are some
who still believe in the "black art." Among the
negroes in this country there are many who are
superstitious in this respect, and a London paper
of June, of this year, says that on the African gold
coast fifty persons were lately burned to death for
witchcraft. Missionaries are slowly teaching the
barbarous nations better. Another use is to enable
us to understand allusions in literature. In Shakes-
peare's plays, for instance, witchcraft is often men-
tioned; and the beautiful poem by Whittier, the
Witch's Daughter — Mabel Martin — could scarcely be
understood by one who had not read some account
of the trials for witchcraft in New England. A third
use is to render us cautious how we trust too posi-

tively to what we believe and do at the present day. It is conceivable that, three or four centuries hence, mankind will read accounts of how criminals were tried, found guilty and punished in our day, and will think them almost as strange and senseless compared with the better ways which will then be known, as trials for witchcraft now seem to us.

WIDE AWAKE.

RECENT AND CHOICE BOOKS FOR S. S. LIBRARIES.

By E. A. Rand.

Pushing Ahead, . . .	$1 25
Roy's Dory, . . .	1 25
Little Brown-Top, . .	1 25
After the Freshet, . .	1 25

By Margaret Sidney.

The Pettibone Name, . .	$1 25
So as by Fire, . . .	1 25
Half Year at Bronckton, .	1 25

By Pansy.

An Endless Chain, . .	$1 50
Ester Ried Yet Speaking, .	1 50
New Year's Tangles, . .	1 00
Side by Side, . . .	60

By Carrie A. Cooke.

To-days and Yesterdays, .	$1 25
From June to June, . .	1 25

By Marie Oliver.

Seba's Discipline, . .	$1 50
Old and New Friends, . .	1 50
Ruby Hamilton, . . .	1 50

By Mrs. S. R. G. Clark.

Our Street, ...	$1 50
Yensie Walton, . . .	1 50
Yensie Walton's Womanhood,	1 50

By Mrs. J. J. Colter.

One Quiet Life, . . .	1 25
Robbie Meredith, . .	1 25

Soldier and Servant, by Ella M. Baker, ...	1 25
Keenie's To-morrow, Jennie M. Drinkwater Conklin, . .	1 25
Hill Rest, by Susan M. Moulton, ...	1 25
Echoes from Hospital and White House. Experiences of Mrs. Rebecca R. Pomroy during the War, by Anna L. Boyden, .	1 25
Not of Man but of God, by Jacob M. Manning, . . .	1 25
Cambridge Sermons, by Alexander McKenzie, . . .	1 50
Self-Giving. A Story of Christian Missions, by W. F. Bainbridge,	1 50
Right to the Point. From the Writings of Theodore L. Cuyler, .	1 00
Living Truths. From Charles Kingsley, ...	1 00
For Mack's Sake, by S. J. Burke, ...	1 25
Little Mother and her Christmas, by Phœbe McKeen, . .	1 00
My Girls, by Lida M. Churchill, ...	1 25
Grandmother Normandy, by the author of "Andy Luttrell," .	1 25
The Snow Family, by M. B. Lyman, ...	1 00
The Baptism of Fire, by Charles Edward Smith, . .	1 25
Around the Ranch, by Belle Kellogg Towne, . . .	1 25
Through Struggle to Victory, by A. B. Meservy, . . .	80
Three of Us, by Heckla, ...	1 00
Breakfast for Two, by Joanna Matthews, ...	1 25
Onward to the Heights of Life, ...	1 25
Torn and Mended, by W. M. F. Round, ...	1 00
That Boy of Newkirks, by L. Bates, ...	1 25
Th Class of '70, by H. V. Morrison, ...	1 25
Uncle Mark's Amaranths, by Annie G. Hale, . . .	1 50
Six Months at Mrs. Prior's, by Emily Adams, . . .	1 25
A Fortunate Failure, by C. B. LeRow, ...	1 25
Carrie Ellsworth, by M. D. Johnson, ...	1 25
The Pansy Primary Library, 30 vols., ...	7 50

***LOTHROP'S SELECT S. S. LIBRARIES. The choicest, freshest books at very low prices.

ADMIRABLE TEMPERANCE BOOKS.

The Only Way Out, by J. F. Willing, ...	$1 50
John Bremm, by A. A. Hopkins, ...	1 25
Sinner and Saint, " "	1 25
The Tempter Behind, by John Saunders, ...	1 25
Good Work, by Mary D. Chellis, ...	1 50
Mystery of the Lodge, by Mary D. Chellis, . . .	1 50
Finished or Not, ...	1 50

*****Messrs. D. Lothrop & Co.**, Boston, also publish the celebrated PANSY AND PRIZE BOOKS. Full Catalogue sent on application.